HIS NAME WAS TOM

The Biography of Tom Rees

by

Jean A. Rees

Jean A. Rees

HODDER AND STOUGHTON

LONDON SYDNEY AUCKLAND TORONTO

HIS NAME WAS TOM

Wyse,
Shady Rill.
Shalvells Rd.
Milford-o-Sea

Contents

Illustrations

ILLUSTRATIONS

Key to Acknowledgments
1 *Sevenoaks Chronicle*
2 Upper picture, Keystone Press Agency Ltd
3 Keystone Press Agency Ltd
4 Both pictures, Keystone Press Agency Ltd
5 Baron Studios Ltd

HIS NAME WAS TOM

CHAPTER ONE

The Countdown

THE consultant in his white coat watched thoughtfully as his patient left the room. This would probably be his last visit. 'No need to tell him,' he said to himself, 'he's prepared for it.' A doctor becomes accustomed to the uncertainty of life. Men like this patient were rare, but his countdown had started.

That evening Tom sat in his room writing his diary. For the last forty-one years, ever since he embarked on what is termed 'full time Christian service', he had kept a diary. He wrote:

February 17. Rose at 6. Prayed until 9. Am greatly enjoying learning 2 Timothy, the only book of the New Testament (except Revelation) that I do not know by heart. Saw the consultant at 11.30. Have angina. Must reduce, walk more, and take some pills. Had a committee on 'Time for Truth'.

Justyn and Joy flew off to British Columbia today. Guide them Lord. He will do a flying job, and then may take over from me in three years' time. God give me strength.'

Tom did not know that the countdown had started, but even if he had known he would not have altered his programme. The consultant did not think it necessary for Tom to go about with the sentence of death upon him—we all have to go some time.

'Rose at 6. Prayed until 9.' His diary for that February day was typical. Rising early was no problem for him. He woke early, and prayer was his delight, a warfare, a time of communion and intercession. Like Wesley, he felt that as he grew busier, he must pray longer.

A few years ago a young man who had grown up with us in the same circle was visiting our home. He told us over coffee: 'Of course, I've got over that old bondage about the quiet time, early prayer, and all that.' Tom listened in silence, then said, 'If it's bondage, I pray I may never be free.' He meant it. I have his prayer list, returned to me with his effects, a slim, black loose-leaf book. Opposite each page is a hymn such as:

> *Jesus, confirm my heart's desire*
> *To work, and speak, and think for Thee;*
> *Still let me guard the holy fire,*
> *And still stir up Thy gift in me.*

He knew these hymns by heart, and as he walked from our home to his office at six in the morning, he would recite and pray:

> *O that in me the sacred fire*
> *Might now begin to glow,*
> *Burn up the dross of base desire,*
> *And make the mountains flow.*

On the day the countdown started, he prayed for himself, for the fruit of the Spirit, for revival in his own soul, for a burden for prayer, for his family, and for the daily programme. There were prayers for Hildenborough Hall, the residential conference centre which, for twenty-five years, was part of his life work. Everyone was covered, from the members of the business executive, each member of the staff, over twenty-five of them, and future projects—a new games room, capital needs, new staff, a colleague to help him personally. Other people are listed, not yet Christians, for whom Tom was praying. There is a page with the names of twenty-five people who were ill, thirteen who were old, most of them over eighty, and one over a hundred. As on all Tuesdays he prayed for China, Japan, and Korea, and for several missionaries whom he knew. He prayed for his elder brother Dick, and for my elder brother Colin, and a host of others.

'I am learning 2 Timothy.' Tom maintained that anyone could learn by heart if they only took ten minutes a day conscientiously. He learned and meditated, read the text in several versions, and was able to quote at length.

When we lived at Frinton, he and I would set out for our 'bodily exercise'. I went to the golf course while Tom set off along the sea wall to walk to Clacton. 'If you would only learn to relax, you could be playing when you are over eighty,' he told me.

'If only you'd *play* golf,' I told him, 'you might be playing golf at eighty.'

He laughed. 'Why spoil a perfectly good walk by having to stop and hit a silly little ball?'

He could just recite the book of Romans on the journey there and back. In his favourite chapter 3 he advanced past Great Holland, getting a bit bogged down in chapter 6 and 'O wretched man that I am' in chapter 7 as Clacton approached. When he turned like a horse scenting corn, he was having a great time in chapter 8, 'No condemnation ... Who shall separate us from the love of Christ?—peril, nakedness, sword?' and by the time he got to 'All things work together for good' all his anxieties were falling off. When he saw me struggling in a bunker at the seventeenth, and slicing down the eighteenth, he was commending Phebe in chapter 16, and saying kind things about Priscilla and Aquila, and was ready by verse 16 to greet the brethren with a holy kiss—or rather the sister.

'Have angina.' He may not have realised how bad it was. Many have angina and live for years. He must have been tempted to share the joke with me. Five years ago, Tom developed diabetes. It was not surprising, as his grandparents on both sides had the disease, and beyond causing exhaustion and a restricted diet, he did not take this too seriously. I had a chronic heart—we both had our 'thing'! Then three years ago I told him I thought I had diabetes too. 'Oh, no you don't,' he said. 'That's *my* "thing". I'm not having you horning in on it.' He must have wanted to tell me that he was 'horning in' on my 'thing', but he was too unselfish. He did not mention it.

I am sure he did not know that the countdown had started. Shortly after, he was doing the mysterious things he always did in early April about income tax. He was going to the States as usual from Easter to Whitsuntide. I said, 'You must tell me what you do for the accountant, as I might be a widow some day.'

'I'll tell you next year,' he said.

The diary talks of 'Time for Truth'. Tom had a concern and grief about the spiritual decline and fall of our nation. Every day fresh signs of the lowering of moral standards caused him literally to weep and pray. With the inspired slogan 'Time for Truth', suggested by David Boulnois, Tom planned to lead a call to the nation.

Before Tom was twenty, in May 1931 he wrote: 'The Lord is telling me that He wants me to be His witness and win many souls. I have it laid on my heart that God has chosen me to cry against this whole nation.'

This was fulfilled over and over in London's Royal Albert Hall and throughout the country, but this burning desire recurred in Britain's present plight. 'Time for Truth' was yet another urgent call to cry against the nation. This programme was not carried out. God said to King David, when he had superb plans to build the temple, 'It is enough that it was in thine heart.' David had collected material, but the temple was built after his death.

As Tom was writing his diary, Justyn and Joy were flying to British Columbia. They had been married three years, and had a baby daughter. Justyn, a trained commercial pilot, planned to start a flying job searching for bush fires. His heart was in the work at Hildenborough, and although we had considered his joining us immediately, taking over the youth programme, we all decided that this should be delayed for three years. It would be better for Justyn to carry out the ideas that he and Tom had discussed when he was in charge, and we had retired.

Tom's diet was rigid; he hardly ate enough to keep a self-respecting sparrow alive, let alone a large-framed man working a seventeen-hour day. We often had tea together, the one oasis in a day that started at six and rarely finished before eleven at night.

'After "Time for Truth" we're going to have a long holiday, no meetings, no work—nothing,' Tom said.

This year, 1970, was 'the year of the insurance'. Most people have a goal or a carrot in their lives. Some talk about 'when we get Aunt Agatha's legacy' or 'when we sell that bit of property', but with us it was the year of the insurance. Tom had paid into it for years, and so we planned after 'Time for Truth' to go to Florida.

When Tom was too tired to discuss work, we talked exhaustively about whether to go direct to Miami, or via New York—what books we would take to read aloud, how we would eat lunch at the Sea Horse Tavern, and buy broiled chickens from the delicatessen! It would be heavenly just by ourselves. With time to talk, we could discuss what to do in three years' when Justyn returned from Canada, and how we would have a retirement bungalow with Tom's tool shop, and my studio in which to paint.

'God give me strength,' said the diary. Tom realised what a challenge it would be in his present state of health to continue for three years at the tremendous pressure needed to carry both evangelism and conference work. I was concerned with his increasing exhaustion. From January 1st, 1970, I dedicated all the time I was in the car to praying for him. As I stepped in, it became a habit—'And now Lord, for Tom. . . .' As well as for health and strength, I asked God to give him the power to

15

pray, a love for souls, spiritual power, and an anointing of the Holy Spirit for the coming task which obsessed his thinking and praying.

During the countdown Tom took only a few big meetings and services, but he was able to lead a number of people to Christ individually. He had the greatest joy in what he called 'the craftsman's work'—helping individuals.

A feature of Hildenborough that had developed over recent years was the unadvertised special weekends when we all brought personal contacts, business and professional men and women, who were not yet committed Christians. These were an outstanding success. Two such weekends were held during the countdown. A doctor and his wife, both over sixty, were deeply moved, and opened their minds and hearts to God. An alcoholic who was trying to find some higher power to keep him from drink, found Christ was that Power. He and his wife became Christians that weekend. Events of this kind were a very real feature of Tom's last years. At one, twelve men accepted Christ, all of whom had Christian wives.

The weekend before Easter, Tom and I considered having a weekend away together. I was to speak at a lunch near Eastbourne, and he wanted to visit someone needing help. In the end we decided it was too expensive. Hotels cost so much, and we would just be content with some hours off in Brighton. If we had known, we could have spent a little of the insurance money in advance. We did not know, but enjoyed walking in the famous Brighton 'Lanes' hand in hand, visiting antique shops, Tom buying old silver spoons to give to his various American hostesses in the six places he planned to visit.

It was fun. We had both stayed in Brighton to write books years before—Tom, a volume on the Person and work of the Holy Spirit, *The Spirit of Life*, while I had written my first novel about a physiotherapist. We had a lovely dinner, and characteristically checked the final proofs of 'Time for Truth' down to the last comma! Tom seemed to have a great sense of well-being, knowing something was accomplished.

Easter weekend came with all its opportunities, and after giving hours in personal interviews, as well as bringing Easter messages, Tom set off in the Jumbo Jet for New York. I wasn't worried about him. So much was planned for September that it seemed only logical he would be back.

For some years now Tom has visited six different American churches between Easter and Whitsun, developing Home Bible Cells, talking to members, visiting their sick, and discussing local problems. As the final countdown continued, he visited old friends and made new ones. His friend, Schuyler English, had arranged his first tour in the States thirty years before. From then Tom loved the American people, and their warm-hearted enthusiasm, describing his annual visits as a shot in the arm that kept him going another year. I had a letter from 'Sky' (a writer and an editor) who tells me:

Tom Rees walked into my office for the first time on May 5th, 1937. My initial impression of him, quite young then, has never altered, but rather my esteem for him increased over the passing years—friendly, warm, responsible, forthright, dynamic, dedicated to, and on fire for Christ. Tom's radiant personality and bright testimony won the hearts of the Americans from the beginning. He possessed spiritual commonsense rare in so young a Christian. His mind was open to new methods of promoting the Gospel, not sensational methods, but effective ways of attracting men to the message. Above all, Tom was a man of prayer. He not only spoke about prayer—he prayed. As I look back upon over thirty years of friendship and fellowship with him, one thing stands out prominently; I never failed to receive a benediction from our visits together.

My last recollection of Tom Rees was when he turned to say good-bye to me after a luncheon engagement. [This, by the way, was on April 11th in Aldan, Pennsylvania.] Only moments before I had gripped Tom's hand, I said, 'Tom, I have reached the age that when I part from friends I feel impelled to remind them that this might be the last time on earth we shall see each other face to face, but we have the wonderful assurance that we shall meet again in Glory.'

Tom replied: 'You're looking quite fit, Sky. You'll be around for a long time.'

Nine days later Tom himself was taken into Christ's presence.

On April 11th Tom writes in his diary: 'Saw the moon blast-off at 2.15.' The memory of the astronauts reading from Genesis, 'In the beginning, God . . .' while hurtling round in space, thrilled him.

Tom's countdown continued, but this was of a heavenly astronaut whose destination was not to see part of God's creation; not to visit a planet, but a countdown for a journey that would take this astronaut right into the Presence of the Creator Himself, who would meet him not only as a Creator, but as a Friend and Master.

Tom wrote every day, sometimes twice, and his brief blue airmail letters gave me crisp information and the never-failing assurance of his love, appreciation and prayer. From Niagara: 'At 3 a.m. I had a vivid dream' [he very rarely dreamed]. 'It was the 5th September, 1970, the opening meeting of "Time for Truth". The place was packed, and I got up and made my opening speech. I went through it all word for word. I was greatly helped, and there was great power. I ended up quite overcome, with the words, "May God have mercy on England." I woke up, and got out on my knees and prayed.'

Every letter writes of excitement about our holiday. 'I have booked the apartment, sent the deposit, and am living for it. Roll on September 30.'

Tom was staying in Richmond, Virginia, and on his last Sunday he preached four times, spoke to some students, and managed to fit in a visit to the widow of an old family friend. His hostess described him as 'jolly and relaxed, telling British jokes to our daughter'. The service was broadcast, and Tom admitted in his last letter: 'I had the wind behind me.'

His hostess recalls: 'He appeared in excellent spirits and mentioned on two occasions that the reason he was in such good form was, " he had received two letters from Jean". He told us from the pulpit that you write every day, and what a wonderful wife he had.'

Tom started on his final flight to New York. That morning, a Monday, he would have prayed the verses in Charles Wesley's hymn:

> *I would the precious time redeem,*
> *And longer live for this alone,*
> *To spend, and to be spent, for them*
> *Who have not yet my Saviour known;*
> *Fully on these my mission prove,*
> *And only breathe, to breathe Thy love.*

> *Enlarge, inflame, and fill my heart*
> *With boundless charity divine:*
> *So shall I all my strength exert,*
> *And love them with a zeal like Thine;*
> *And lead them to Thy open side,*
> *The sheep for whom their Shepherd died.*

He would have prayed for his friends Stephen Olford, Billy Graham, and Leighton Ford. While flying, he wrote over seventy postcards, including one to 'Chick'. The previous November we had visited Chick's home. His wife, Mary, was about to have heart surgery, with three new valves to be inserted, and there was a very slender chance for her recovery. Mary wasn't worried; she had trusted Christ six years ago through the ministry of my sister, Lois, who had visited and cared for her, but Chick just would not, could not, accept Christ, in spite of being ill with lung cancer himself. Tom talked with him for hours. Later Mary had her operation and recovered, but Chick remained in darkness. Tom sent him a card from the plane, saying he was praying for him every day. When the card arrived Chick was in hospital. His wife Mary was able to lead him to the Lord, and saw the fear go from his eyes. He is now with the Lord.

I have a letter written on his last day. He was exuberant over the successful return of the Apollo 13 spacemen.

Did you see the landing of the spacemen? As soon as they landed on the deck, the ship's captain said, 'I have asked our chaplain to say a word of thanks to our Heavenly Father for bringing our lads back safely.' They all took their hats off in silence, and a super extemporary prayer followed. It was most moving! I hope the B.B.C. let you see or hear it. I preached four times yesterday. Had the wind behind me. Shall be following your plans all the time in prayer. Am phoning Justyn and Joy tonight at 9.00. Just landing. Love Tom.

I had watched, as did the whole world, the anxiety over the precarious trip of Apollo 13. Like every happily married woman I had wondered what the wives were feeling: what an awful thing to lose a husband! How could anyone bear it? Of course, I should have remembered (I have since) some advice Ruth Graham gave me: 'He never gives grace for anticipated trials.'

That morning Tom would have learned his verse for the day. By learning, he could meditate, and at odd moments he always repeated his verse, two verses together, so that he could link them. He was learning 2 Timothy, chapter 4, verse 7: 'I have fought a good fight, I have finished my course, I have kept the faith.' He usually put a thin pencil line down the side as he learned. The line finished at verse 8: 'I have finished my course ... Henceforth there is laid up for me a crown of righteousness.'

He arrived at the Salisbury Hotel, built over Calvary Baptist Church which is filled week by week with those who come to hear Stephen Olford. He planned two days' rest at the

Salisbury where he could spend his last day with Heather who, as a little girl of ten, had accepted Christ when he was preaching in Ireland; when she was eighteen, he had been instrumental in inspiring her to dedicate her gift of playing the piano to the Lord. At Hildenborough she had met Stephen Olford.

Tom unpacked and wrote, 'Phone Justyn at 9.00'. He stuck it up in a prominent place while he and Heather went out for a meal together. At dinner they talked mainly of 'Time for Truth'. The whole idea possessed Tom's being. Twenty-five years before, Heather had played the piano for him in the Westminster Central Hall, London, where the services were to be held.

What was in Tom's mind as he thought of the verse he had learned that day? He always checked it with other translations. Phillips puts it: 'As for me, I feel that the last drops of my life are being poured out for you. The time of my departure has arrived.'

They returned to the Salisbury. Tom said he was a little tired, and would leave his coat and come up to Stephen and Heather's apartment for coffee. As he left the elevator at the sixteenth floor, he would go back to his verses. 'I have fought a good fight ... I have kept the faith ... I have finished my course ...' He put the key in the lock of the apartment. He went in, and no doubt saw the reminder that he was to phone Justyn that night.

When a soldier knows he has finished his battle, he *lays down* his sword, but Tom was in the full flight of battle—he *hung up his sword*.

'I have kept the faith ... Henceforth there is laid up for me a crown ...'

GLORY!

CHAPTER TWO

The Adventure Begins

A STATION MASTER in the mid-nineteenth century was a very important personage. He wore a top hat, a frock coat, and greeted each train with dignity. The first French primer I read in the third form describes the scene at the station: '*Le chef de gare se promène majestueusement sur le quai*,' which I learnt meant: 'The station master walks majestically on the platform.' So did Tom Rees's great-grandfather, Richard Rees, in the little town of Carmarthen. To be a station master in the nineteenth century was something, but to hold such a position on the Taff Vale railway was superb, for his special privilege was to hand to each passenger a copy of the Bible to be read during his journey.

Richard Rees's son, Richard (there was always a Richard in the family) did not follow in father's footsteps, but went to seek his fortune in the big world, and having, like so many of his descendants, found it irksome being an employee, founded his own business in the City of London. This was a dressmakers' wholesaling business, Grandfather Rees being the middleman between the dressmaker and the manufacturer. He invented a rather vital part of the hook and eye that is used to this day, and became increasingly prosperous. Even though he never acquired the dignity of the '*chef de gare*', he certainly 'promenaded himself' majestically around his Berkshire estate, to the admiration of his grandson, Tom. Tom gained his interest in running a large estate, as he watched Grandfather Rees go round the greenhouses, the peach houses, vineries, walled garden, and rose gardens. He would go with the chauffeur to meet the launch at Pangbourne. Grandfather Rees did not believe in all work and no play, and rounded off his return from the City by travelling in his private launch to the landing stage at Streatley. He wore a top hat and frock coat, as did Tom's father, another Richard, who followed in his father's footsteps, and never called his father anything but 'Sir' or 'The Governor'. Grandfather Rees never failed to conduct family prayers, and Tom as a small boy could recollect the moment when the staff filed into the dining room and Grandfather Rees, in a sonorous voice, read the Bible and prayed. He preached regularly at the Countess of Huntingdon chapel in Goring. He was a man of wide vision and interests, and could keep his grandsons enthralled about the stars, show them fossils, and interest them in archaeology.

It sometimes happens that a clever man passes on his ability to his son. Richard Rees, Tom's father, was one of the kindest men, of great integrity, but compared with his father, of limited ability.

Pop, as everyone called him, not irreverently, but in affection, followed rigidly in his father's footsteps. What was 'good enough for the Governor was good enough for him'. Unfortunately, when he inherited his father's prosperous business and considerable fortune, he did not realise that the Governor would have moved with the times, reinvested wisely, and used the advice of a skilful accountant. Everything the Governor had done was sacred, and it never occurred to Pop that possibly the reason why the success of the business plummeted, was that modern dressmakers, and other customers, did not admire the advertisements of Victorian ladies with eighteen-inch waists and bustles. What was good enough for the Governor ... The business dwindled and ground to a halt, and 'riches took to themselves wings'.

Tom's maternal grandfather rose to the top of the police

23

force, and after becoming the equivalent of Gideon of the Yard, retired in his mid-forties, and bought a farm. The house had been the birthplace, hundreds of years before, of the only Englishman, Nicholas Breakspear, to become a Pope of Rome. Tom's grandmother, Anys Bonner, mother of thirteen children, never called her husband anything but 'Mr. Bonner'. Her family name was 'Wake', and they could proudly show their descent from Hereward. Grandma Bonner became a Christian when Moody visited London, and sang in Sankey's choir.

The wisest thing Pop ever did was to marry Florence Ada Bonner, a woman of great physical beauty and enormous natural charm. Had Tom been brought up by his grandfather, he might have been spared the inhibitions of a child whose mother has to double for both parental roles. Pop, having begotten three sons, and given them the unimaginative names of Dick, Tom, and Bill, had no idea that he had any other responsibility. Dick, Tom's older brother, had been easy to train, but Tom received rather rigid discipline, was infected with a horror of dirt, untidiness, and natural accident, and this helped to make him the fastidious perfectionist he became. During those early years, tolerance rather than corporal punishment might have been more helpful. Tom was completely devoted to his mother who, when the need for discipline lessened, became a delightful companion to her sons, arranging parties and picnics, dances and fun with complete abandon. Tom will never have the sorrow of losing his mother. I have her with me, still as much fun to be with as ever, and looking like a duchess.

Every mention of Grandfather Rees showed Tom's satisfaction in him. I have heard him describing Christmas Day. They all arrived the day before, for an almost Dickensian scene; Grandfather Rees reading the Christmas story at morning prayers, then taking the service at the Goring church. After that came the presents, and the Christmas meal with real gold sovereigns in the Christmas pudding!

Tom's introduction into the great world of education filled

him with horror. At the age of five the rather apprehensive small boy was introduced by his mother to the schoolmistress who ran the kindergarten school. Tom had always embarrassed his mother in buses by exclaiming in horror at any ugly face, and Miss Bunbury completely horrified him. He buried his face in his hands, and said in a low voice, 'Oh, Mummy, isn't she ugly.' Poor Miss Bunbury might have done something about her moustache, but the enormous wart by her nose was a fixture. Tom watched it every day with fascinated horror, and was totally unable to open his mind to anything she said. In the end, almost in tears, Miss Bunbury asked Tom's mother to remove him. 'He does nothing but stare at my wart,' she said, 'and won't learn.' Fortunately his new teacher was more pleasant.

At Watford Grammar school Tom was, we must sadly admit, a dull boy, well behind his age group. All through his life he said his favourite number was 415, because school ended at that time, whereupon he went straight round to the big railway junction in Watford, and could describe intricate details about engines and their construction. One master at school seemed to understand Tom. This was the games master, Stanley Rous, now Sir Stanley, and famous in the world of sport. 'School is no use to this boy,' he told Tom's mother. 'He has a good enough brain, but will learn better on his own.' So, very sensibly Tom's parents, having in a most progressive manner checked with a psychologist, took Tom away from school, and he went to work in the City.

With the restraint of school gone, Tom threw himself into a life of riotous enjoyment. He was a born leader, looked a great deal older than his age, and at sixteen was proud to be taken for twenty. He and his crowd went to dances, shows, and parties. These were in no way orgies and extravagances, his chief sin being that of living for himself and the fun of the moment. Tom did not smoke or drink. Pop, like 'the Governor' before him, had promised him a substantial cheque if he neither smoked or drank alcohol until he was twenty-one. This bribe was successful with all three sons.

Tom enjoyed life in the City. His friend Arthur Willis, who worked with him, described Tom as tall, good-looking and fair, but very shy and awkward. Fearing he would be tongue-tied with the waitress, he practised his lunch order at Lyons—'Roll and butter, piece of cheese, two Swiss buns, and a glass of milk.' All this for four new pence, which was as well as he was earning the magnificent sum of £36 a year.

Life at 'Llandyssul' in Bushey, Hertfordshire, must have been great fun. Tom's mother made the home not only happy but full of enjoyment. They were a wonderfully united family. Then Dick, the happy, extroverted Dick, became a Christian. It made a division, for his standards were new, his interests different. He broke it to the family that he wanted to become a parson. Pop approved of that; he was an ardent churchman, sang in the choir, and with his wife was a keen supporter of the church whist drives and dances, although 'old Dick' as Pop called him, disapproved of the whist drives and dances.

Tom was scornful, and with a rapier tongue never missed an opportunity to mock 'Dicky the Deacon'. 'Dear Brother,' he would say, 'Have you had a blessed time?' Dick smiled his famous gappy smile. In 1926 Dick 'ruined' all Tom's winter programme of fun, and did so deliberately. He got a number of his friends, including the Church Army Sister, Ida Stubbings, to covenant to pray for him every day until he became a Christian. Suddenly Tom began to suffer from deep depression. He was moody with Arthur, didn't think he was funny any more, was irritable about the dances, and failed to turn up, walking around the lanes thinking of the utter futility of life. How angry he would have been with Dick if he had known about prayer missiles that were 'ruining' his life.

On New Year's Day, Tom went off alone weighing things up. He knew very little of Christianity, he read no books; he had hardly any knowledge of the Bible. But he knew he needed Christ to take over his life. With a great effort that hurt his own pride, he knelt by his bed and committed his life to the Saviour. He knew nothing of the meaning of the atonement, but he did know that his life was under new management and the only thing to do was to act on that. He went to Dick's room, where his elder brother sat studying. If ever he felt foolish, it was then. Dick didn't look up, but went on writing, so Tom said, 'Dick, I want to tell you, I've—I've become a Christian. I've asked Christ to be my Saviour.'

Tom stood by ready to catch Dick if he fainted, but Dick took off his glasses and said quietly, 'I'm not surprised.'

'You're not *surprised*?' asked Tom. 'I thought you'd faint!'

'Oh no,' said Dick. 'You see, I've been praying, and I expected an answer.'

Dick lost no time in telling Sister Stubbings, who had prayed for him.

Fortunately for Tom—and many who have helped through his ministry since—Sister Stubbings had no inhibitions about dealing tactfully with the new convert or of breaking him in gently. As soon as she heard of his conversion she sent him a message to say she would expect him at her children's meeting to assist. Tom meekly agreed to go, expecting to give out hymn books or help to keep order. First he must buy himself a Bible.

Tom had never read the instructions to employees in Ephesians—'Be obedient ... not with eye service as men pleasers, but as servants of Christ', but on January 3rd (I had this from Arthur Willis who was there), Tom arrived at work *on time* and started at nine, even though the boss did not arrive until nine-forty! Genuine consternation among his colleagues. They gazed at him and said, 'What's the matter?'

'Nothing,' said Tom. 'It's nine o'clock.'

'Come off it,' they said.

'I'm paid to work from nine,' said Tom.

'Look here, what's all this? What's the big idea? Out with it.'

Tom realised he would have to tell them. They gathered round.

'Last night I became a Christian; and—well, I just feel it's

27

the right thing to do, to work when I'm supposed to, whether the boss is here or not.'

Derision and mocking applause greeted this. Tom of all people! Arthur mocked most of all, his quick wit cutting Tom to size. There was astonishment that afternoon when Tom returned from lunch with an enormous new Bible.

He turned up at the children's meeting like the little oyster, 'all eager for the treat'. As he arrived, Sister was teaching a new chorus. When she caught sight of Tom, she said, 'Now, boys and girls, we'll sing the chorus once again and then Mr. Tom Rees is coming up here to tell you how he became a Christian.'

Tom's heart turned over! Clutching his new Bible for support, he made his way to the front. He showed them his Bible and told them what it meant to him now.

After the meeting, Sister asked, 'What are you doing on Saturday?'

'Saturday?' asked Tom. 'I always go to a dance on Saturday night.'

'Don't waste time on things like that now you're a Christian; there's work to be done. You'd better come pubbing with me. We'll visit the workhouse first.'

Tom meekly agreed. He went with Sister to the workhouse, and then to thirty of the town's public houses, giving out Christian literature. It wasn't long before his natural organising instincts asserted themselves and he started organising Sister!

'Why can't we do more for these men than just give them tracts? We ought to open a coffee room for them.'

So they did. They had a slogan for their coffee room—'If you want the joy of joys, come along and join the boys!' At that time Tom was not the coffee making expert he later became, but some were too drunk to know its flavour!

Tom visited the workhouse each Saturday afternoon, taking pots of jam and honey to the aged inmates and reading the Bible to them. At the first prayer meeting he attended in his life, before he had been a Christian a week, Sister announced: 'Now

Mr. Tom Rees will lead us in prayer.' Everything is easier after the first time, and Tom said that is why he was often ruthless with new converts in making them pray as soon as possible. Sister asked him to speak at a young people's meeting. Tom had no idea what to speak on, so he made a start with predestination and free will!

Sister suddenly asked him to read the Scripture lesson. This had been one of his mental blocks at school, where to read aloud made him break out in a cold sweat and be unable to cope. The inevitable sarcasm or shrug of exasperation made matters worse, but now when he got up with his new Bible, he found he could read with ease, no longer tongue-tied. From then he gave his mental abilities totally to the Lord, and found that what he read he retained, and although he would never be an academic, yet he would 'Study to shew himself approved unto God, a workman that needeth not to be ashamed' (2 Tim. 2:15).

The rebel disappeared. Gone was the purposeless, pleasure-loving Tom; he became an exuberant, enthusiastic young soldier, with an almost overwhelming call to share his faith with others.

One day, after having his picnic lunch in St. Paul's Churchyard, Tom heard a lecture in the Cathedral. 'Woe is me if I preach not the gospel,' he heard was round the skirt of the big bell called Great Tom, and he took this as his motto.

During the first few weeks of Christian life, he not only spoke to everyone about his faith, but was successful in leading people to Christ. By the time he had been a Christian one month he knew of over thirty who had accepted Christ, many from the crowd who had shared all the fun. They banded themselves under the name of Pro Deo, and this group of young people who were 'For God' experienced a miniature revival. As with the early Church, the Lord added daily to them other converts.

Before Tom's conversion he asked one of Dick's friends: 'Why must you people be such miseries—you don't do this,

and don't do that. Why can't you be a Christian *and* have
fun?'

'Why don't you become a Christian and show us how?' was
the retort.

Tom did just that, and while going in wholeheartedly with
every Christian activity, if time permitted he saw nothing
incongruous in going to a prayer meeting in his dinner jacket
and going on to a dance.

On a crowded dance floor he told his partner of his new
found faith. 'Since I saw you last I have become a Christian.'

'You have what?' she asked.

Tom repeated it. She stood stock still, took her hand off his
shoulder, and said, 'Then what the hell are you doing here?'

Her plain speaking shook Tom. He soon found that what had
once delighted and entertained him became boring, while his
work for God was thrilling and exciting.

He seized every opportunity of speaking in the open air in
his own home town of Watford. He and his crowd took over a
Sunday school with twenty children attending, and seventeen-
year-old Tom, without experience of any kind of Sunday school
work—he had never attended one himself—became the
Superintendent, and the teachers were his own converts from
the Pro Deo group. They kept 'one lesson ahead of the pupils'.
Soon there were two hundred children. There was no shortage
of teachers, for there was no shortage of new converts.

CHAPTER THREE

Finding the Way

Tom left the City to train to be an estate agent, but the desire to preach was oozing out of his finger ends, and the invitations to speak, and the opportunities to do so, crowded in upon him. Suggestions were made to him by many helpful friends who recognised his gifts. One was to go to Canada with the Colonial and Continental Church Society, but the invitation that appealed most was from the Rev. E. L. Langston, Rector of Sevenoaks. He needed a youth worker to take on the Sunday school and the youth work. Sevenoaks and the Rev. E. L. Langston little knew what was going to hit them when the suppressed energy of what Mr. Lindsay Glegg later described as the 'atomic Tom' made its impact upon them!

St. Nicholas Church, Sevenoaks had a strong evangelical tradition, and recorded the names of former rectors in an almost unbroken line since the twelfth century. Mr. Langston, a little man with a great evangelistic heart, was a good preacher. He had more super-tax payers than any other parish in England! To Tom, everything was black or white. People were either saved or lost, and if the rector considered that some things might be grey, this to Tom was almost compromise. His diary reads: 'The Bishop preached. Lord, Thou canst save even Bishops!'

After earning only £36 a year, £150 per annum seemed riches. He settled in digs with Miss Millis, whom he called

31

'Diggle Darling'. She was a patient woman. Before long Tom was inviting masses of schoolboys to tea, whom she entertained quite free of charge. Even more wonderful was her patience over Chang, Tom's great dane, a clumsy but endearing dog, whose delight at Tom's return greatly strained the endurance of Miss Millis. The lead of this enormous animal one day became entangled with the grandfather clock, and when Chang bounded at his master, down came the clock, knocking over china and glass ornaments.

Tom's work included visiting parishioners old and young, rich and poor, hospitals and almshouses. He loved the old people.

A rich man living in the parish had had a desire to do something for youth, and with local co-operation had built a magnificent hall, started a Sunday school, and then found he was totally unsuited for the leadership. The Sunday school was completely out of hand, the young people did as they liked, and the benefactor was disheartened. He said to the rector, 'Find a man who is a disciplinarian and has experience with young people and ask him to take over. I'll pay his salary and give him a free hand.'

Tom's first job was to tackle the Sunday school where there was bedlam. The children who would have liked to listen were unable to do so and numbers had dwindled. The ringleader was a boy of about ten, a 'holy terror', from a difficult home, who had no respect for anyone.

The first day Tom went to the Sunday school he told them that in future he was the boss, and if anyone talked or misbehaved they could go home. He announced a hymn amid silence. In the middle of the hymn the 'holy terror' made an observation to his friend. Tom stopped the hymn and told the boy to go home. It was a shock to all; the rest of the school behaved like angels, and for the first time for weeks listened to the lesson.

Tom found the address of the boy and visited the parents, telling them that he could return to Sunday school when he

The Rees boys, Tom, Bill, and Dick.

Tom at camp with Boadicea, his first car.

Some of the boys from Banwell.

Tom (*left*) at eighteen with his new Bible, and (*right*) Arthur Willis, his old sparring partner in the City, now a minister in Prince Edward Island.

Tom on Sandpulpit at Swanage between Captain Reginald Wall and Rev. W. G. Owens.

was willing to behave. He returned and behaved. Tom took the choir boys for an outing to the coast. On the way home in the train this boy lit up a cigarette. Tom told him to put it out. The boy went on puffing. There was a struggle and the cigarette went out of the window, amid a torrent of foul language.

Mr. Langston must often have suffered at the sight of Tom, eager and enthusiastic, inclined to say 'Hallelujah' at the wrong time!

'Mr. Langston, I've got a wonderful idea,' Tom told him on November 30th, 1930. 'How about some texts outside the church? What a witness that would be!'

Tom in his enthusiasm would have chosen something really pungent, such as 'The wicked will be cast into hell' and 'Prepare to meet thy God!'

Years later Tom said to me, 'Poor Mr. Langston, I know now how he felt'.—We were sitting in Cardiff, parked behind a car which was stuck in the tramlines. Impregnated in the actual paintwork were just such texts. On the boot was 'Behold, I come quickly' which caused riotous Welsh humour.

In November 1930 Mr. Langston prayed for grace. Tom's diary records that he explained it would 'make the church look like a mission hall, and we shouldn't cast our pearls before swine. The Church Council wouldn't like it.' Tom mentioned in his diary a few of the swine—citizens of whom the rector was afraid. 'Personally I think it is withholding bread from dying souls. Lord, if I'm wrong in these things, forgive me. If not, open Mr. Langston's eyes.'

Tom had strong convictions. 'I had to help with a sale of work. I am strongly against sales of work, but I am working for Mr. Langston, and I must do what he says.'

Not long after the text incident he writes: 'I am very downcast tonight and sorely tempted to leave Sevenoaks because outside the church there is an advertisement for a concert. Maybe the swine did not mind the concert, even if the texts might have got under their hairy skins.'

His inner life shows conflict, sometimes despair, often discouragement. The diary pages are a letter to the Lord, with the devil as scornful onlooker. Before he was a Christian he did not believe in the devil, but never doubted the existence of God; after his conversion there had been the occasional question: 'Is there a God?' but he never doubted again the existence of his old master. 'Do I believe in the devil?' he would say. 'Of course, I used to work for him.'

His diary starts on the 5th November, 1930—'Rose at 6.00, spent time in prayer. Went to the Parvis (a little prayer room at St. Nicholas Church) at 10.15 to pray.' The next day he writes: 'The devil gained a victory today, did not rise until 8.20. On November 10th the devil tempted me not to trust Him about my future, and then again on November 12th the devil won the battle of the bed, but praise God he did not win the battle of Calvary.'

Tom was learning the lesson he handed on to many teenagers. 'Buy an alarm clock,' he said, 'and when it sounds, seize the blankets, and say, "Depart from me ye workers of iniquity" and leap out of bed.'

Mr. Langston tried to persuade Tom to be ordained. 'Mr. Langston says he wants me to study under him, and he will get the Bishop to ordain me. He says it is all right for me now, when I am young, but when I am older, my zeal will wane. God forbid. May it wax and wax. How I am longing to preach to "lost hell-bound souls" ... The enemy has made me very depressed today about my future. I expect he's depressed about his future, the bottomless pit, and the lake of fire! Praise God, I am more than conqueror through Him.'

His prayers acquired a growing maturity. After an entry where he visits a poor widow who has lost her husband, he goes to the hospital to visit two newly converted boys. 'God grant me more of Thy Holy Spirit that Thy love may flow deeper through me.'

After a hectically busy day doing Sunday school business, he writes: 'Lord, visit us with Thy salvation, and teach us that our

34

busyness is not business. I feel I would like to go headlong into the stronghold of the devil. Visited some of the rich people in in the parish.'

It was not all mountain top. On November 16th he tells us: 'My spiritual power is very low. I have been guilty of laziness. I am nothing, and have no power of myself unless I pray.' Things were worse two days later. 'The devil has the victory again. Read about the lost axe head, lost by disobedience and neglect of prayer. I've lost it, and must go back for it. It's no good chopping with the axe handle. Lord, save thy servant from the enemy, for I am weak, but Thou art mighty. I was greatly helped to triumph by musing on Ephesians. Lord, accept my thanks. I am very weak, but Thy strength is made perfect in weakness.'

One after another senior schoolboys, and older people, became Christians. Bunny Loughlin was Tom's first convert; Railton Michaelis, a sensitive schoolboy, became a soulwinner in spite of persecution. One day he found the Bible Tom had given him ripped in pieces. John Speed-Andrews, Alan Staines and Sid Saker are all ordained ministers today, and many others are on the mission field.

When Tom arrived at the Bible Class one day a boy was playing the piano. Tom instantly recognised his ability. Peter Letchford just played for fun, by ear. 'You should study music, you could be a great pianist,' Tom told him. Peter today has a B.A. in Classics at Oxford plus his B.Mus. After years as a missionary in Africa he became the pastor of one of the most successful community churches in the American Eastern States. Tom comments on Peter in April 1931: 'If Peter keeps humble, faithful, obedient and prayerful, God has a great future for this boy. The whole of the Classical sixth are now converted and have lively prayer meetings.' Tom found that when Peter played, he could sing (his Welsh blood coming out), and they became so at one spiritually that after preaching Peter was ready at the piano for Tom to sing an effective message, 'You must do something with Jesus', with the challenge 'No

neutral ground must be taken, you must do something tonight';
or 'He whispered "Peace be still" to me' brought a hush of
expectancy. A typical comment in Tom's diary said: 'Sang
"Can others see Jesus in me?"—personally I doubt it!'

Although Tom was learning to be sober, his young converts
were irrepressible. As the Church Lay Worker he took many
Scripture lessons with the senior boys, and these studies in
Exodus laid the foundation of his Bible Studies from Egypt to
Canaan.

The headmaster was disturbed by Tom's influence and asked
him to explain why the boys in the senior classes thought it
necessary to put texts on the inside of the teacher's desk, and
the desks of fellow pupils. Tom suggested it was better than the
pin-up girls the other boys displayed. It was hard to face the
Classical sixth, open your desk, and be told about the wages of
sin!

God was kind to this young soldier fighting with outward
enthusiasm, but secretly wrestling with the world, the flesh, and
the devil. His old sparring companion of the City, Arthur
Willis, came as a companion in the fight. There was mass
unemployment and Arthur needed a job. Mr. Langston
suggested that Arthur could work in the vicarage garden and
in the parish youth work. Miss Millis agreed to take him as an
extra lodger. After much manoeuvring and string pulling, Tom
persuaded Mr. Langston to appoint Sister Stubbings as the
Church Army Sister to St. Nicholas. She too was accommo-
dated with Miss Millis.

Tom now had a fellow worker, and best of all someone to
pray with. He writes: 'Arthur Willis came and we spent some
hours in prayer, the happiest I have spent for a long time.
Arthur and I prayed again in the Parvis, and I am exercised to
pray that souls will be saved. This is the first time for weeks
that I have *felt* the Lord's presence while I have prayed.'

Having prayed, Tom is very excited to have an opportunity
for aggressive evangelism. 'Miss Clark (later our dear friend
Kathleen Walkden) has invited me to lead a Boys' Camp. She

is a very spiritual woman. How I would like to do this. I must pray about it for I am very unworthy.'

Although outwardly so confident, the diary reflects the undercurrent of shyness. 'I went to a New Year's Party at the Y.W.C.A. There were forty women and young girls. I felt so nervous.'

On January 12th, 1931, Tom writes: 'In the afternoon Brother Willis and I went for a walk and talked about our Christian life, and came to the conclusion that our sin was laziness. We arranged to meet at the Upper Hall for prayer at 7.15.'

Alas, for the best made resolutions, when 'Brother Willis' arrived at 'Brother Rees's house, he was still in bed at 9.00 a.m. 'Lord, forgive me,' Tom prays. 'Spoke to the boys on "Temptation, and how it can be overcome". I felt such a hypocrite.'

He makes some serious New Year resolutions. 'I have made the following resolution, not because I want to, but because I know the Lord bids me to rise up every morning of my life at 6.00 a.m. When the alarm rang at 6.00 I was tempted to go back to bed, but these two verses rang clearly in my ears—"I have opened my mouth unto the Lord, and I cannot go back", and "Endure hardness as a good soldier." '

For good measure he added another resolution which he never failed to fulfil, even if the blankets and the devil sometimes won the battle of the bed! 'The Lord has been speaking to me about my slackness in the stewardship of my money. I shall d.v. get a book, put down how I spend His money, and from today forth give a tenth of my income to the Lord.'

He was already contributing ten shillings a week towards the expenses of Arthur's keep, and half a crown a week towards the Church Army Sister's pay, but his tithe account became part of his way of life, and so when, many years later, he wrote his book *Money Talks*, and discussed teenage pocket money, students' grants, wages, salaries, legacies and first fruits, he knew what he was talking about.

On January 27th the Lord continued teaching him. 'Spent

the morning in prayer. Arthur and I came to the conclusion that it was useless praying for revival in our lives if we are not obeying Him, so we went to the Parvis, and told the Lord we would obey Him at all costs.'

To round off the day they went to hear the Rev. C. J. B. Harrison who told them, 'The reason why so many great preachers become powerless is because they begin to think they *are* something.' This seems to have caused Tom a burst of further prayer: 'Lord, save me from ever sinning in this way.'

Did his landlady's carpet suffer like the one in his bedroom at home? When he left for Sevenoaks his mother said, 'Perhaps now I can get a new carpet.' His bony knees had worn two holes by the side of the bed!

It seems not surprising to read on January 30: 'A fruitful day. Heard of two young men named Smith who were converted today, and Railton told me of his friend who had come to Christ. This is the third soul I have heard of today. I prayed that never another Sunday night might pass during my whole life without my speaking for the Lord.'

He still believed in fasting, as well as prayer, but this resulted in some soul-searching. 'Felt there was too much Tom Rees in my preaching. Had a day of fasting again. Diggle says I am mad, but that's what they said about the Lord.'

In February 1931: 'The Lord has said to me lately, "You have been putting too much of Tom Rees into your preaching; the message was all right. It was My message, but not delivered in My Power." The Lord promised me, "If you can only lean back on Me, and don't trust your own eloquence, your preaching will be changed."' Every penny he could spare was spent on books.

In the mid-century years, when nearly every winter Saturday Tom was preaching in the Royal Albert Hall, as we motored up on the A21, passing masses of coaches with stickers saying 'We are going to the Albert Hall to hear Tom Rees,' we passed a mission hall in Dunton Green. Tom invariably pointed out that this was the place where he had his first mission. The Superintendent said, 'There has been more done this last week than in the last ten years.'

On May 5th he wrote: 'Have been hearing the Lord's Will calling me to more method in my life, more discipline. Spent much time reading Spurgeon's *Lectures to his Students*. The call persists.'

Sister Stubbings, not given to flattery, told Tom, 'The Lord has told me that you will be an even greater soul-winner than Dr. Torrey.'

He held a camp for thirty-six slum boys from London, and prayed that all would be converted. His prayer was answered. On July 2nd he comments: 'Miss Kathleen Clark, the Secretary of the recruits department of the Church Pastoral Aid Society, came to see us at 11.00. She said it was the cleanest Camp she had ever seen.'

Even the tent pegs were scrubbed! That was typical of Tom's attitude to Christian work. Nothing must be slovenly, only the best was good enough for God. It was the first of many such camps. The following year Tom took a number of boys from Sevenoaks with him. The 'holy terror' who had tried to wreck the Sunday school became a Christian. He is a gifted minister today.

Four boys from London who attended the camp had started work and had to leave early. Tom had noticed that they had not enjoyed the meetings. When they came to say good-bye, Tom asked them why they had not enjoyed the camp. They protested loudly that they had, but Tom persisted and faced them with the fact that they had not accepted Christ. They looked a bit awkward, then the leader said: 'Yes, sir, you're right. But you don't know how tough it is where we live and work, and we've talked it over and decided that we aren't going to become Christians at camp, because we couldn't keep it up.'

Tom was speechless for a moment, then, stretching out his hand, he said, 'Harry, hold on to me for a minute, and whatever happens don't let go.'

Harry put out his hand and gripped Tom's wrist.

'Now promise you won't let go,' Tom said.

'I promise, sir.' Tom gave a sudden jerk and wrenched his hand free.

'Now, let's try again,' Tom said, but this time he put his hand round Harry's wrist and gripped it like a vice.

'Now, go on,' Tom said, 'get free.' But he pulled and twisted in vain.

'It's no use—I can't, sir.'

'But why not?' Tom replied. 'We came apart the first time—now we seem to be stuck. How's that?'

'That's quite easy, sir. First time I had 'old on you; now you've got 'old on me.'

Tom explained that being a Christian is not so much our holding Christ, as Christ holding us. The next morning, while the porridge was cooking, the lads told Tom that they had given their lives to Christ.

At one of these camps a boy came to Tom, having torn his trousers. Tom offered to sew them, and while he sewed, he led him to Christ. As the boy went away, Tom remarked that it was a good thing he had torn his trousers. A few weeks later Tom received a letter:

'You will remember me; I am the boy who came to Jesus through a hole in his trousers!'

CHAPTER FOUR

Preparation for Life

In the last months of 1930 Tom writes: 'My late master, the devil said, Tom, you will never be able to preach because you can't get up enough sermons. I reminded him that I would not get them up; I'd get them down! ... O how I long to have the privilege of preaching the gospel of the grace of God. Had the pressure of the Gospel message oozing out of my finger tips.'

'On December 2nd the Lord gave me a message on "The Rich Young Ruler", the thoughts straight from Himself. Hallelujah! The Lord saved six to eight souls.'

But on December 3rd he writes: 'I feel very fed up today. The Rector called. I asked if I might be free to go out and preach on Sunday evenings. The answer was "no".'

Mr. Langston would rarely have the opportunity of hearing Tom preach, and would not realise his urge to preach was being justified in his performance. For instance, on the final night of his first evangelistic mission at Dunton Green, Mr. Langston felt he ought to preach himself, not even sharing the service with Tom, who writes:

'I was very amused. The Lord chose me to lead the mission, but on the last night I was invisible! The organ blower failed, and Mr. Langston said "My Lay worker is here, he'll blow the organ". Praise the Lord and hallelujah.'

Little things happened to keep Tom humble. He writes:

'I was a little hurt. The curate organised a Coffee Evening

41

for the upper classes, dinner jackets and all that, but I wasn't invited.'

About this time Tom realised he might as well sell his dinner jacket and buy a few more books.

We who are living in the 1970s must try to understand how different things were in the 1930s. Today, anyone can obtain a grant, but between the wars, unless parents could pay high fees, training presented a real problem.

The whole thinking of Christian people today has radically changed. Then there was an urgency, time was short. The imminence of the Second Coming of Christ was stressed, and the arms race was on. Those who left their secular occupations to give their whole time to evangelism (as distinct from regular ministry) did so without the present-day desire for a training to fall back on, and a job with a pension. Particularly on the mission field today it is the man in a secular occupation who has the unique opportunity of doing missionary work, but in the thirties for a man to go back into a secular job, having had the call to whole time service, would have been considered putting the hand to the plough and going back.

The day of the pioneer without qualification has gone. We thank God today for those who went into battle sacrificing ordinary careers. Let us remember that had Ian Thomas not left his medical career, there would never have been Capernwray Hall and its seven offshoots. Let us remember Alan Redpath who left accountancy; Roy Hession who left a secure position in the bank; Stephen Olford whose agile brain could have won him high honours. All these entered the arena of fighting evangelism. I am speaking of those whose calling was to be pioneers.

Thank God for hundreds who were able to train the minds and dedicate their lives. Today it is of the utmost importance that Christian men should gain the highest qualifications, not for their own aggrandisement, but because today qualification counts so much. What a highly qualified scientist says about religion is listened to with awe, even though the compliment is not returned, should the Archbishop of Canterbury give his opinion about space travel!

Tom's training was disciplined and thorough. He believed in the apprenticeship method. He took every opportunity not only of hearing great preachers and evangelists, but of making copious notes. No medical student walking the wards with a gifted surgeon ever observed more keenly than Tom did when listening to Lionel Fletcher; watching the gifted song leading of Arthur Wood; the rhetoric of Dr. Sangster and his predecessor Dinsdale Young, giants of Methodism. He sat under the spell of Lindsay Glegg, whom he describes in his diary, in 1932, the first time they met, as 'the sanest Christian man I have ever met'. Later there was Dr. Ironside of Chicago and Dr. Barnhouse of Philadelphia. In his impressionable teens and early twenties a little of all these great men rubbed off, and he in his turn at Sevenoaks took his young converts with him, and taught them to lead singing, to preach, and lead men and women to Christ.

'He didn't teach us only Christian things,' one of that group recalls. 'He knew that some of us would go to the University, into the Church, and yet knew nothing about ordinary social conventions. I remember his taking us to London, not to Lyons, but to a large hotel, where in those days one could have a seven course meal for five shillings. He casually explained to us the mystery of the cutlery. "Let's all start working from the outside and work in," he told us, and without realising it, he got it across that we broke our roll, and didn't cut it!'

Tom revelled in books. At one time after preaching for a week he was given three whole pounds! The reaction was typical: 'Was able to send 10/- to Sister Doris and bought a Young's Concordance for 30/-.' Every book he bought was precious, whether it was Dr. Scroggie's *Fascination of the Old Testament Story*, or Bishop Ryle's *St. John's Gospel*. When he first came to my home he stood 'astonied' in front of my father's bookcases.

'You've got all these books in your house,' he said to me.

'What a Bible student you must be.'

I'm still ashamed thinking about it! Tom went on digging all his life, reading, studying, finding out the origin of words. He was not a student by nature, would never have won a scholarship, but he was totally dedicated. He used to say, 'If I can study, anyone can.'

The first mention of his lesson in trusting God for material things was on November 12th, 1930. He writes: 'We need a piano. Found a beauty for £5. O Lord, open the hearts and pockets of Thy people.' His personal needs too he brought to the Lord. 'Bought a suit £3. 8. 3. Need an overcoat. Help me, Lord, to sell some of my old clothes to get the £3. 12. 0 I need.'

A friend, a junior partner in a famous pen manufacturers, asked Tom, 'What will you do when you want to get married? You'll have no money in this sort of a job.' Tom writes: 'The Lord gave me the reply. "If I look after the Lord's business, He'll look after mine."'

I do not think the idea of being married had entered Tom's head. He was convinced that it was better for an evangelist to remain single. Girls do not feature in his diaries. They seem to have vanished along with the dancing and gay life.

Imperceptibly a certain apprehension creeps into the diary. 'For some time I have been afraid of living a life of faith depending only on God, not having a fixed income, relying on Him for all my needs, because it is such a worry to keep praying about food and clothes.' The mood passes. 'How silly I am to be fooled by the devil. God has told me that if He calls me to this sort of a life—and He may do—there will be no need to worry. He will not fail.'

In spite of his courage and God's provision, from time to time there is a wistful note. In June 1931 he writes: 'I met my friend George who has just bought a motor bike. He is in business. I felt rather sorry for myself, because I have done what I believe is the Lord's Will, and have not a penny to spend, and he has all these things which appeal to me as a young man. Then the devil tempted me and said: "Your people are spending all that money on Dick. They are paying £30 a term for this College, and soon he will be earning £6 a week as a curate. He will get married and have a home of his own, and the way you're going on, you'll never have a penny to bless yourself with." ' Then he writes: 'Praise the Lord, the devil is a liar. The Heavenly Father has given me the verse—"Seek ye first the Kingdom of God and His righteousness, and all these other things will be added unto you." '

Tom continued in much prayer about his future. Various evangelical societies offered him jobs, but he had no guidance concerning them, and still resisted Mr. Langston's urge for ordination. A crisis was brewing.

CHAPTER FIVE

The Emerging Evangelist

THE mission at Dunton Green gave Tom his taste for evangelistic missions with its night by night preparing, preaching, praying and fasting; so when he was denied the opportunity of preaching on Sunday nights, and an invitation came from Seal for a ten day mission, he was delighted. It never occurred to him that it was incongruous for a lay worker from the parish church to preach in a local Baptist mission hall. Had he not done so in Dunton Green and held the closing meeting in the Anglican church, with not only Mr. Langston's blessing, but his presence as preacher?

But Tom had to learn that all Anglican vicars were not so ecumenically minded. The Vicar of Seal heard of the preparation for the mission in his parish. The fat was in the fire! On November 12th Tom went to see him, as an act of courtesy rather than to ask for permission. When Tom admitted his identity, the Vicar exhibited the appearance of one about to have a fit!

'You come to preach in a Baptist mission hall in *my* parish when every day I kneel down here and pray that we may be saved from such rank non-conformity. Everyone who attends that place has departed from the mother church.'

The Vicar continued, 'We must be born by the water of baptism into the holy church, which is the Body of Christ.'

Tom writes: 'After telling him that when, *if ever* he gets to

46

heaven, he will get some surprises in finding non-conformists there, I mused on the way home. What shall I do? Why should souls go to hell just because the Vicar refuses to let me go?'

In riper years Tom would have been a little wiser with the Vicar. He goes on : 'Can I hear David say, "Goliath, please may I sling a stone at you and cut off your head?" Lord, is it Thy Will for me to hold this mission? If it is, I will go. It seems very important for me to go to Seal.'

But now, the fat was not only in the fire, it was sizzling! Mr. Langston was very worried. He sent for Tom and asked him characteristically, '*Now* what are we going to do with you?' He showed Tom a letter from the Vicar of Seal.

'Dear Mr. Langston,' it read. 'Your lay worker tells me he intends preaching in the Baptist Chapel here. Surely you can find enough work for him in your parish without interfering with me and encouraging non-conformity.'

If Tom wasn't as wise as a serpent, certainly the Vicar wasn't as harmless as a dove!

'There's going to be trouble,' Mr. Langston said, breathing heavily, looking a little bleak. 'I'm afraid he will complain to the Bishop, and it will all come out.'

'What will come out?' asked Tom.

'All about you,' he said in a low voice. 'He'll find out that you've not been confirmed.'

Tom understood—how tolerant Mr. Langston had been to accept him as a lay worker though he was not confirmed.

Few knew that when Tom had attended confirmation classes, he was asked to say that it was in his baptism that he became regenerate and was made a child of God, and an inheritor of the Kingdom of Heaven. This was too much for him. He had been converted a few weeks ago, and refused. With great understanding, Mr. Langston had not pressed the point.

Mr. Langston did face trouble with the Bishop, but Tom, quite determined to go to Seal, made his big decision. He resigned as lay worker at Sevenoaks, but promised to continue as an honorary youth leader until the way opened for both his future, and a substitute for him at the parish church.

The Rector shook hands. 'I honour you for being true to your convictions,' he said, and the crisis passed.

Tom never forgot what he owed to Mr. Langston.

He has a comment in his diary: 'Took a party to Weald in Mr. Langston's car. Unfortunately smashed it up. He wasn't cross, which showed his really victorious life.'

When Mr. Langston was over eighty, and was living at Beatenburg, Tom always made a great effort to visit him. I asked him why, when he was so terribly busy, he took time off to travel so far to see Mr. Langston.

Tom said, 'I always hope that when I am a widower and over eighty that perhaps Oliver Styles or Ian Cory will come and visit me and give me encouragement.'

On January 1st, 1932, Tom writes: 'Spent the last moments of 1931 confessing past failures and praying for 1932. Hallelujah, and thank God I am now free to do the Lord's work. I am reluctantly going by faith. After paying bills I step out on £12.'

As Tom launches out he prays: 'Dear Father, I have staked my all on Thee, have Thine own way. All I ask is that Thou wilt glorify Thy Name by saving souls in these last days. God grant that I may walk humbly with my God the walk of faith in the path of obedience.'

His mother wrote: 'I'm not worrying about you, I feel you are doing the right thing.'

The devil, of course, had his word to say: 'Tom, don't be a fool, you don't know anything about the Bible; no one will ever ask you to take a mission, so go back into business, and earn an honest living.'

Tom throws a reply: 'Thank you, devil, advice is more often given than taken.'

Tom had strong views about living by faith, and was insistent that it ceases to be a life of faith wholly dependent on God if anyone knows about it. He kept his way of life to himself, and even Peter Letchford, his close friend, had no idea that Tom's

house from which Tom and I were married, (*left*), and where Jennifer was born.

Tom's parents at their Golden Wedding.

On board the *Queen Mary* with Rev. E. L. Langston, Kathleen (Jean's sister), Montague Goodman, Jean, and Tom Rees.

Christmas 1942 in our Elizabethan cottage during the three happiest years of our life.

£150 per annum had ceased before the Seal Mission. Living the life of faith, Tom often said, can degenerate into a spiritual confidence trick, if over advertised.

For financing evangelism he followed the example of St. Paul, who made the needs known to Christian people, suggesting a collection.

So Tom kept his own counsel, and it was a wonderful exercise of faith in his training. 'Take no anxious thought for clothes,' Tom writes on February 18th. 'Have bought a new jacket and trousers. Lord, send me the 56/- I need.'

Every supply was a miracle. Quite frequently he was down to his last five shillings. At Waterloo Road Mission, after a week's preaching, he refused the five pounds offered him, saying: 'Three pounds is enough.' He knew they were short of funds.

When I first met Tom, a group of us invited him to speak at a drawing room meeting, and I gave him a cheque for two pounds. He asked almost rudely, 'What d'you want me to do with this money?' I said, 'Well, haven't you a fund or something for expenses?' He brightened up: 'Of course,' he said, 'I'll put this to expenses.'

For some reason—I think he inherited this from his Grandfather Rees—he always gave the impression of having plenty of money. I had more as years went on, but he would never let me give him anything. 'I'm not meant to have money,' he said, 'I'll tell you if I'm short.'

His brother Dick says that he and Bill always called Tom 'our rich brother'. When asked why, knowing Tom had so little of his own, Dick says vaguely, 'I suppose it's his clothes.' Tom spent an absolute minimum on his clothes, in spite of always managing to look well dressed. He sent them to a special cleaners who not only pressed and cleaned, but mended and sent them back just like new.

Just before he died he ordered a new pair of shoes, hand made, very expensive, and as this was such an event, he told me about it. 'It's the first time I have had a new pair of shoes for fourteen years,' he said. 'I wonder how many pairs of shoes *you've* had in the same time?' Of course, he made his usual joke that he had 'trees' in his shoes for twenty-four hours—T. Rees in the daytime, and shoe trees at night! He wore his shirts one to twelve in sequence; consequently they all wore out at the same time. He had just had some new handkerchiefs. The last time was for his trousseau thirty-four years before!

Tom would have loved the good things of life, and before he was thirty had many invitations from both Canada and the States that would have enabled him to have them. He could have served the Lord and prospered financially. 'How would you like me to be the Pastor of a church with a salary of £15,000?' he asked me once. 'For part of the year I would be free to preach and do conventions, and would earn another £5,000.' We both agreed that £20,000 out of the will of God was not to be compared with the peace of mind of serving God. Some people are called to serve in prosperity, and some in comparative need. Both are right if they are doing God's will.

The mission at Seal, which first started Tom on the life of faith, was not a roaring success, and did not start a vast revival in Kent and throughout the nation. Things do not happen like this. It was a quiet mission, and very thrilling things happened on a small scale.

Tom had the wind behind him at Seal even if he did not realise it. Running true to form he records: 'On the first night the electricity failed and the service was conducted by candle-light (like a Holy Mass). A child was sick, but on Sunday a young man came up and said he had become a Christian.'

The convert, who became Tom's life-long friend and colleague, was Oliver Styles. Oliver had been persuaded against his will to attend that Sunday. He imagined it would be peopled by old ladies listening to an evangelist of white-bearded vintage. He could hardly believe the atmosphere of gaiety. There was Peter Letchford at the piano, Phil Saker with a flute, and Sid Saker on the violin. Oliver was astonished to find the speaker was very little older than he was. He says: 'When Tom began to lead the service I was stirred by his brightness and happiness. He was fully confident, completely dedicated, and eager that others should share his faith. He threw himself completely into the task of leading, preaching, and singing. I was impressed too with the others on the platform.'

The message gripped him, and for some unknown reason, and urged by power outside himself, he turned against the swim of people, and gripped Tom's hand. Tom immediately roped him in for service. On the Friday night he gave him an invitation to go 'pubbing' with him. Tom had urged him to come to the seven o'clock prayer meeting—'Make sure you pray,' he said, 'I'll be waiting for you.'

For the last forty years Oliver's life and service have proved that the mission at Seal and Tom's step of faith were justified. Oliver is so like Tom in his orderly way of life. He sent me recently some of Tom's letters to him over the years. His first letter to Oliver just after his conversion says: 'I am sending you a copy of *The Spirit's Sword*. Spend at least half an hour with your Bible each day, and you'll become strong in the Lord. I have been praying that God will make you a soul-winner.' This prayer was answered. Thousands of men, women, and particularly children, have been converted under Oliver's ministry. Like Tom, he is still a layman. He worked first with The Caravan Mission to Village Children, with us at Hildenborough Hall, and on many evangelistic crusades, and with the Scripture Union. Tom, not yet twenty-one, signed his letter 'Christian Greetings, Yours sincerely, T. B. Rees.'

On September 5th 1934 when Oliver was going to college, Tom wrote: 'Go on, and be on the offensive when you get back to college. Remember you're not sent to keep peace, but to drive the enemy back. Let's disturb the slumber of his satanic majesty . . .'

His letters continue with odd bits of advice, such as 'Make Him your object, even more than souls,' but of course Tom was never more thrilled than when he heard of the souls won by his beloved son in the faith, and he often said, 'I see you're still at it, Oliver, making me a spiritual grandfather!'

Every man of God must go through the classes in God's school. The secret pages of his diary show the problems, disappointments and frustrations that prepared Tom to be a man of God. Occasionally he was allowed sudden success. On November 4th, 1932, Tom had his first taste of preaching to large crowds. Dr. Martin Watney rang him at four o'clock, and asked him if he could catch the boat train to Belfast to preach there. Tom packed and caught the train for Euston in less than fifteen minutes, and then went by boat train to take charge of one of the centres in a city-wide mission headed by Lionel Fletcher. For six days Tom preached at Crumlin Street Presbyterian Church. Nearly two hundred were converted, including a channel swimmer and a minister's son.

During a later Ulster mission Tom wrote: 'God has taught me to pray during this mission. 160 out at the early prayer meeting. Spoke on Romans. As we were praying I wondered what it was brought so many folk together so early. My personality? No—a thousand times no. Nothing but the Holy Spirit operating through a man learning to pray.'

Thousands of Ulster people thank God for his visits, and owe their salvation to these missions. The campaigns in Ulster were a training ground for him. He said, 'I feel I can pray the moment I put my feet on Ulster soil.'

The Ulster missions were Tom's school of evangelism. He learned the value of speaking to Christian people first, on practical living and effective praying. At Lurgan, one of his earliest, a shopkeeper was mystified to find three people paying debts of long standing. He asked the third person why. 'I expect they were at the mission last night,' he was told. 'If you have bills owing, that's a sin, and God can't bless,' Tom had said.

To see four hundred people up praying on bleak winter mornings was very thrilling, especially to hear the prayers that said, 'Thank you for saving my sister . . . husband . . . son last night.'

Tom had a horror of anything deceptive in evangelism. 'I

have no use for china eggs,' he often said.

The Rev. John Speed-Andrews, one of the boys from Dunton Green and Seal writes: 'The moment that stands out with me at Seaford, and was a great help to me in my evangelistic work, was this. One of the team asked Tom if it would help at the cinema service if, when the public appeal was made, he would go forward to break the ice. Tom said emphatically, 'On no account. The one who has to break the ice has the greatest blessing. Don't rob him of it.'

Joyce Silcox, Tom's secretary, working with me on his biography, recalled that she was converted at fourteen in that cinema, and she was the first to go out!

In Ballymena the senior schoolboys and girls, afraid of being crowded out, came straight from school to the church, brought their homework, and reserved the whole block for their schoolfellows. What Tom described as 'a very healthy number' committed their lives to Christ.

Do these teenage converts last? Mr. Percy Matthews who arranged the follow-up of the mission has the cards signed by teenagers. Years later he could account for the majority—'He's a minister today—she's out on the mission field—those two are married and have a Christian home.'

Tom learned not only the joy of success, but the exhaustion and fatigue that goes with it. In one of his Belfast missions he wrote: 'Came in very tired. I was attacked by his satanic majesty thus—"You were defeated; you were just saying that God is working out His purpose." I read to the devil from Exodus 5:22, "And Moses returned unto the Lord, and said . . . why is it that thou hast sent me? Since I came . . . to speak in Thy Name, Thou hast not delivered Thy people at all. Then Jehovah said unto Moses, Now shalt thou see what I will do to Pharaoh . . . I am Jehovah." With a fainting heart,' says Tom, 'I prayed as Moses did, and God renewed and strengthened me.'

Later the devil assured Tom—'You're making a fool of yourself. Give up these meetings.' Tom had learned from Christ to reply by Scripture: 'And I said, And now, Lord, behold his threatenings—Grant unto Thy servant boldness to speak Thy Word, stretching forth Thy hand to heal, that wondrous things may be done in the Name of Jesus.'

Prayer seems to have been answered when he addressed about 1,400 people in Belfast: 'The largest crowd of people I have ever preached to. There was great power. The minister's daughter was converted; also a mother of ten. Two of her daughters accepted Christ during the past week. This mother was about to leave the hall when she came face to face with one of her sons—"What, you here too?" And they fell on one another's necks and wept.'

CHAPTER SIX

'Til Death us do Part

AT the time when Tom was converted I was living in New-castle. My parents with their seven children moved to London in 1927, the year Tom became a Christian. My father was born in the Victorian age, and had a Victorian outlook. Although he was no Mr. Barrett of Wimpole Street, he had a tremendous personality with a great belief in 1 Timothy 3:4 (One that ruleth his own house, having his children in subjection). He had joined the Brethren as a young man, but although his head held many strong convictions about separation, his heart was full of love for evangelism and the Lord's people everywhere. Although he was very busy in the firm his Grandfather founded, at one time he preached every night for two years, and hundreds of people were converted in Tyneside, so when I met Tom, evangelism was nothing new to me.

My upbringing was different from Tom's. Whereas there were few prohibitions or restrictions in Tom's home, we were brought up to be 'separate from the world'. Mother and Father made us feel special. People who only lived for this world, poor things, had to have something to cheer them, whereas what waited for us one day was so glorious that it would have been cheating to go to the picture house and see Charlie Chaplin in *The Kid*. We decided ourselves what we did on Sunday, but when there was a houseful of people to entertain, and hymn singing after tea, there was something positive. What fun it was, all singing in parts, and happy laughter. We did things together, whereas Tom's brothers each had their own rooms and own interests. When there are seven there is always a four for croquet, someone for ping pong or tiddlywinks. But we just did not live in a permissive society. I had never been to a film or theatre, and so great was my desire to serve the Lord utterly, that I gave up reading fiction, even the kind I now write! I prayed each day that I would never marry. I wanted to work in the slums and not take the 'lower line' of marriage. I was the kind of undisciplined person that would have read silly novels and taken life easily had it not been for the driving force of Christ. I wasn't disciplined enough to keep a diary!

To have masses of brothers and sisters is bliss. It is wealth and riches, not materially, but the joy of friendship when we grew up, and the pleasure of nieces and nephews, like extra sons and daughters, money cannot buy.

To secure father as a director in a very large London firm, his business was amalgamated, and we moved to Hampstead. After Newcastle-on-Tyne it was a dream house, a big, cream-coloured building with lawns, old-fashioned trees like mulberries, quinces, walnuts, peach houses, vineries, yet near buses.

At seventeen I lived at home and took courses in a variety of subjects. It was not done to take a job with a salary, as there was so much unemployment. To do so would be taking a job from someone who needed it. I did a secretarial training, had art classes, cookery lessons, all the training I needed for my future life work.

Hoping to work full time in the slums, I ran a weekly women's meeting and boys' meeting in the east end. I spoke at four or five women's meetings a week, and by wearing what many call a 'saved hat' I managed to look a few years older. Into my happy life of dedicated spinsterhood there came the explosive character that was Tom Rees.

I first met him when I was one of a team conducting a holiday mission in Hampstead. We were a very earnest crowd of young people; one was a doctor, another a solicitor who today is a judge, another became a missionary doctor, one a headmaster, and another was a teacher. There was Ian Thomas, now Major Thomas, D.S.O., and there was dear Chris who flew his burning plane out to sea in 1940 rather than bail out and risk killing civilians. Tom was the leader, and leader he was! I described him to my mother as a man of about thirty, very bossy and self-opinionated. Actually he was twenty-two, and the presence of a potential judge, doctors and teachers did not overawe him. His burden was for the success of the mission.

The first evening when we were happily settled for a chat, Tom rose to his feet and said, 'We'd better get off to bed or we won't be able to get up to pray tomorrow.' As he walked briskly away I said to my friend, Margaret Lyon, 'My word, we are going to be bossed about.' I had a terrible desire to stay up till midnight, but somehow one didn't.

Tom and I argued and fought about everything. He told me I was a cross between a film star and a P.B. I resented the Plymouth Brethren label as he told me incidents of what happened to him at a P.B. meeting, and I reminded him about the notorious vicar whose story was in all the papers at that time, who had been defrocked, and was exhibiting himself at Blackpool in a barrel. I asked him, 'Why a film star?' and he muttered about my hair, but never betrayed it into a compliment. We did share a concern for aggressive evangelism, a love of old-fashioned hymns, and a genuine conviction that anyone who had wholly given themselves to Christ was far better to be single.

'I couldn't hope to marry,' Tom told me. 'I couldn't afford it, and even if I could, I would be far freer in serving the Lord alone.' I agreed, and said that to be unmarried was the highest line.

We had a good holiday mission. I was impressed by Tom's dynamic preaching and amazing ability to act the story he told. I thought he was sometimes a little flippant, but when I knew him better I found that he learned to pray that even his chance remarks might be under God's control.

One night one of our party brought a friend for whom he had been praying, a young man from a wealthy home who tried to give the impression that he could not care less about religion. He told his friend in a bored way, 'I'm off tomorrow for a cruise in the Mediterranean.' Tom was speaking on Jonah, and the flippant remark that shocked me was an arrow to the young man's conscience. Jonah was fighting against God, Tom said, but he tried to put a good face on it, and said to his friends, 'Yes, I'm going for a holiday—I'm off on a cruise to the Mediterranean.' The young man went on his cruise a Christian.

My father was impressed with Tom's preaching, although the first time he heard him he waited behind to 'give him a word' and breathing heavily, he said, 'Do you study doctrine at all?'

Outwardly confident, but inwardly terrified, Tom said: 'A little.'

Father said: 'I think you might look into the difference between substitution and propitiation.'

Tom and I continued working together; he ran children's services on the beach, and I ran the girls' camp. We were relaxed because we knew that neither of us was thinking anything about each other—or were we? A feeling came over me that the only person I ever wanted to marry was Tom, but I tried to put it completely out of my mind. Mother and I were always close, and one day I asked, 'Mother, what will I do if Tom Rees doesn't propose?'

The answer came calmly, 'You'll have to propose to him yourself.'

We stared at each other in consternation. 'Whatever would your father think?' she said, and we never mentioned the subject again until the night of November 15th.

Father unconsciously placed young men into two categories; the young men who came to tea on Sunday, whom he fondly imagined did so in order to hear him expounding Romans, and the others who fell from grace and proposed to my sister, and occasionally to me. Father's face was not 'towards them'!

Tom's diary on November 13th records: 'I am spending sleepless nights because I am in love with Jean Sinclair. Here's a problem that worries me. If I really love her, and I do, then there's one thing, and one thing only that I care for as far as she is concerned, her highest happiness and health. If we fall in love with each other we shall not want it to stop there, we would naturally think of marriage. Now, having given myself utterly to the Lord for His work, I have very little to offer any girl, and as Jean has such a wonderful home, she will feel it all the more, so perhaps the best thing for me to do is to run off and keep out of her way; yet there are signs of her love for me. What shall I do?'

On November 15th we went down together to Seaford to look for a house for a seaside mission party next year. Tom was hilarious. At one school he said, 'Let's introduce ourselves as Mr. and Mrs. Rees.' I thought to myself, he wouldn't joke like that if he was serious about me. I was wrong!

As we drove towards the level crossing gates at Uckfield Station, Tom asked (it's in the diary): ' "Do you think there is any danger of our falling in love if we see more of each other?" —There was a long pause, and Jean said: "Does it matter?" "Yes, it matters," I told her.'

Tom went on to tell me about the horrors of marrying an evangelist—no money, separation, hard work. I do remember saying, 'Yes, Tom, but do you love me?' He said: 'Of *course*,' as much as to say, what a silly question to ask. He didn't try to carry me off my feet with emotion. After a hearty handshake I went off to tell mother. Tom's diary comment is choice: 'Jean talked it over with her father and mother. They weren't exactly pleased, but not cross!'

Mother was insistent that I talked to father immediately. It was a strange thing, but neither of them said: 'Do you want to marry Tom Rees?' or 'How do you feel about it?'

I told father, 'Tom Rees has just proposed to me.'

Father had no objection to Tom being, what a good Brother would call 'out on the work', but he realised as a father of seven, that to rear a family as an evangelist, on an evangelist's pay, was difficult. He said heavily—the mental shock must have made him speak before he thought—'Well, you'll have to learn about birth control.'

'Father!' I said, horrified, 'Is that all you can say?'

Father looked equally horrified, and said, 'Don't tell your mother I said that.'

Tom's mother came to see father and mother a day or so later, looking gorgeous as only she could, and being so sensible. Looking round the drawing room at Belsize Court, she exclaimed: 'I am so ashamed of Tom. How could he do such a thing?'

Father fell for her, and they became fast friends.

The only thing Mother didn't approve of was Tom's nose. She was a character expert, and knew whether you had domestic bumps or obstinate chins and full eyes! 'You'll find him very hard to live with, with that long nose,' she said. 'Men like that see everything!' She was right. He missed nothing, but he saw good things too, and possibly expressed more appreciation than a shorter-nosed man.

On the Sunday I got engaged nobody came to tea. Tom was away, and father could not understand that no one was interested in Romans any more.

It is strange that I didn't think it incongruous on returning from my first evening with Tom, after we were courting, to find father standing there with watch in hand. 'Five *past* ten,' he said. 'This is a very bad start!'

Tom was now on the staff of the Scripture Union. I had £120 per year of my own, and we worked out ways and means. We tried to budget our expenses, and to my annoyance I left a note around, 'Food £1, rent £2, clothes ...' I reclaimed the note from a table, and my little sister said, 'Father saw that.' Very embarrassed I asked, 'What did he say?' 'He just said "poor kids",' she told me.

The next day he said he was going to give us a house as a wedding present.

Father, of course, was very sad that Tom did not join the Brethren. With Mr. Langston urging confirmation on one side, and father urging separation on the other, Tom was hard put to steer a middle course, but in 1936 all was set fair for our lives together. We had a great summer programme in mind— Keswick, the seaside services, camps, missions, and a lovely little home in Mill Hill. The only condition father made was that our house must not be more than half an hour from Highgate!

When Tom and I had been considering the wisdom of our working in double harness, while I was still convinced that it was a lower line, he found a verse: 'One of you shall chase a thousand, but two of you shall put ten thousand to flight.' We prayed we would chase those thousands together. Our evangelistic zeal was tremendous. The work was first, our married happiness a bonus.

Then the Lord tested us both. I got a streptococcal throat— a dreadful virus that gave me a virulent rheumatic fever. I was in dreadful pain night and day.

The house was finished, and as May 6th approached I suddenly realised that I was not getting better. My trouble is that the more ill I get, the more cheerful I become! I tried to break it to everyone that I was very ill, quoting Wordsworth when, with my sisters, the bridesmaids, mother and Tom were opening wedding presents. Waving my swollen hands I said:

> *The first to go was little Jane,*
> *In bed she moaning lay,*
> *Till God relieved her of her pain,*
> *And then she went away.*

This was a riot, and I was little Jane for days. I quoted Frances Ridley Havergal—'What, dying, Emily, can it be?' This became a saying. 'I suppose it's "Dying Emily dying",' Tom would say, even in recent years. Then, in desperation, when my sisters were trying on their bridesmaids' hats I suddenly shouted: 'Take those silly hats off—there isn't going to be a wedding next week—probably never.' There was a horrible hush. The doctor confirmed there could be no wedding for some months. It was not until August 22nd that Tom and I were quietly married.

I was in my seventh heaven when Tom and I set off for Lisburn in Northern Ireland on a dreary November day for an inter-church mission. Oliver Styles, our co-worker, was with us.

We enjoyed the afflictions of the gospel which took the form of staying in a Y.W.C.A., so cold and dank that we almost froze hanging over the electric fire, feeding the meter with pennies. After a swearing, drinking policeman was wonderfully converted, the place was alive with miracles. What a joy it was to work with Oliver, as he preached in overflow meetings, to find he was as effective a preacher as his spiritual father.

There was a year of thrilling opportunities ahead. Captain Reginald Wallis introduced Tom to Dr. Barnhouse, who told Schuyler English, 'We must hear this young man in the States.' He invited Tom to occupy his pulpit in Philadelphia while he was at the Keswick Convention. So all was planned, and the cabin booked for us on the *Queen Mary*.

It was wonderful how Tom had developed. The Irish missions had given him experience and deepened his Christian life. Those who heard him there realised that he had the maturity at twenty-four to preach in conferences and leading churches.

I realise now how extraordinary it must have been for Tom's family, and even his young friends, who considered Tom a complete dud, to understand the change in him. The only explanation many could give was that my father had arranged for Tom to go to the States. I was highly incensed when I overheard one of Tom's brothers saying, 'Do you think if I married one of Jean's sisters I could go on the Queen Mary to the United States?'

Wives can be very sensitive and touchy. When the story was told about Tom leaving instructions about the feeding of his dog 'three bowelfuls' I laughed heartily, but was on the defensive. Tom was often word blind, and his diaries can read like Moody's letters home. He often used to ring his secretary, and say: 'Are you by yourself? Well, tell me how to spell "forty". What? Not "fourty"? What a silly language!'

A prophet is not without honour save in his own country. My brothers may have resented Tom for taking me away from them, but they had great respect for him. They almost boosted his ego. They admired him the way he used tools, and was handy about the house, and they loved his preaching, although my younger brother never forgave me for sobering Tom down. 'You've ruined him,' he told me. 'When we first heard him preach we were rolling around with laughing all the time, and now you've spoilt him; last time we only had one decent laugh.'

The fact that Tom was not ordained may have greatly reduced his value in the eyes of his father and Mr. Langston, but increased his favour in the eyes of my father. Tom was growing up, acquiring poise and dignity, but there was a dreadful trial waiting for us, a trial that left a permanent scar on us both.

Over Christmas 1936 I got an attack of 'flu. Although we did not know it then, I had two faulty valves in my heart after the rheumatic fever, and became terribly ill. Even Tom's diary is silent about the worst part of 1937. I was unable to pray with Tom, and the thought of missions, meetings, and going to America was out of the question. I suppose it was nature's way of giving me a rest from the strain of evangelism. Tom had to bear this alone, as I was too ill to share the load with him. I had been taken to my home in Bishop's Avenue.

Tom writes, after quite a gap in the diary in 1937: 'It is hard to pray; indeed for some days I haven't prayed at all, but thank God there is a real desire in my heart to live near to the Lord and live wholeheartedly for Him. Am reading John Wesley's diary.' This reading of the book was one of his life-long tonics.

In April 1937 he writes: 'Took Jean to a heart specialist

who gave us the grave news that her heart is permanently damaged through the illness of last summer. She must lead a quiet life. In spite of this, not because of it, I rejoice in Romans 8:28.' He quoted an old Sevenoaks almshouse woman of nearly a hundred who said, 'The dear Lord knows what He's a-doin' of.'

I was left behind while Tom visited the United States. It was then that Tom fell in love again, a love that lasted to his dying day. He fell in love with America, the American people, their whole-heartedness, and their efficiency. I was to learn to dread saying to Tom when I wanted a telephone number, 'I'll ask directory enquiries.' This would call forth the inevitable, 'In the United States, you would have it within seconds, and now you will have to wait for ten minutes, only for the operator to deny all knowledge of the subscriber, even though it's in their own local directory. They do it so well in the States.'

Tom was to cross the Atlantic forty-eight times, but he never had the desire to live there, for Britain was his mission field.

In 1936 he went to conferences and conventions, including the famous Pinebrook and the broadcast sent out by Erling Olsen, the well-known Wall Street business man. He heard a young man in insurance sing in the programme—his name was Beverly Shea.

His diary tells about his inner testing: 'Am tempted to worry about Jean,' and then, 'Very depressed indeed about the trial the Lord has seen fit to send me.'

My parents were wonderful. Father and I painted; he in oils, and I did my water colours. They just took my illness for granted, and when Tom returned, to his great joy I was ready for the next step on the pilgrimage. It wasn't easy. It was obvious that we must settle down in one place for a time. We thought that our sphere was to be a large mission in the east end of London. Proposals and counter proposals were made for many months, with total disappointment and frustration. Tom thought it was what the Lord had in mind for us. I had always wanted to work in the slums.

It was a time of international tension, of wars and rumours of wars. We were able to visit the United States together, and South Africa, and then instead of the big mission in the east end of London, we were sent to a little village in Somerset, what seemed at first to be the 'back side of the desert'. Not many months after the beginning of the war the area in the east end of London was completely flattened, and in our 'back side of the desert' where we thought we were to minister to a few people, an Air Force camp of fourteen thousand men sprang up, with hundreds of soldiers billeted in the village itself.

CHAPTER SEVEN

The Pastoral Privilege

MY next travels through the diary take me to three of the happiest years of our life. Tom became the minister of the Banwell Baptist church, four miles from Weston-super-Mare, five miles from Cheddar. We left our house in Mill Hill and rented a house with long windows, simple but gracious. Tom had been thrilled with our first home: everything there was what my brothers and sisters called 'very Rees'. I had been proud of my green velvet curtains and window seat to match. One day Tom spilt a glass of water over the cushions. My mother had told us that if anyone spills anything, we should not make a fuss or cause an atmosphere, so in my ignorance I said, 'Don't worry, Tom, it doesn't matter.' Did he think what a nice wife I was? Not a bit of it! He gave me a serious lecture about my lack of concern about property, and that I ought to have minded about the cushions. I thought to myself, 'Just you have one more spill like that, my lad, and you won't know what's hit you!' I think our taste had matured, and we now had lovely patterned linen cushions that would not show the dirt. We were to entertain young people and dozens of members of H.M. Forces, and the home had to take second place.

Our first Sunday in Banwell stands out in my memory as one of total bliss. All the pain, weakness and disappointment was wiped out. We walked through buttercup fields to the lovely little church, and we spent the afternoon together in our new home just revelling in conscious present happiness. Tom wrote: 'With Jean. Talked, walked, sat and read, with Jean.' He seemed to revel in recalling: 'Jean spoke at the meeting to the women and young people.'

We could not get enough of each other's company; if I went out shopping, Tom was there at the gate to meet me, and if I was preparing a meal while he was out visiting, my heart was beating hard, because at any moment he would be home. I know that this is what many people have for years, but we had it in its intensity for three.

Both of us took it from the Lord as a bonus, but we were by no means idle. Tom visited systematically, and we started every kind of activity. It was not only a pastoral ministry, but a continuous evangelistic campaign, in preparation and harvest.

We ran a large children's meeting and spoke at it alternately. One night I told Tom I was going to speak on the boy with the five loaves and two fishes, and he said that next week he would tell about Will's wonderful garden, a story every speaker delights to tell. When I tell a Bible Story I disguise it a little, and planned to talk about picnics, and lead up to the subject, but to my rage Tom read the Scripture in Matthew 19, said a little about the boy and his picnic, and then handed over to me, having completely ruined the dramatic surprise of my story. To his growing consternation I said: 'I want to tell you about a boy who lived in a garden—his name was Will....'

Lionel Fletcher maintained that every evangelist, after working in itinerant evangelism for seven years, should stay as a pastor in one place for three years, and then go back on the road again. Tom realised the benefit as he fell into Mr. Fletcher's pattern, and we realised again that my illness, testing although it had been, was in the plan. The regular preparation of several sermons a week, prayer preparation and follow-up of converts gave the evangelist sympathy and understanding with the men in a regular ministry. It was during those years that we formed our Gideonites. For a mission we were planning one Easter, we formed a group who would pray for three people in the village who were not yet converted. The mission was to be taken by some of Tom's converts and their friends. Peter Letchford was to be there, and the 'holy terror' of Sevenoaks, who was now a vicar! There was almost a revival atmosphere in the village. Strange to say, nearly all those specially prayed for were converted before the mission started, and they in their turn became soulwinners.

Among the most ardent helpers were two men. Bill was a successful athlete, who had become a hopeless drunkard. The friend next door invited him to hear Tom preach. Bill was convinced that Tom had been primed beforehand, because every word seemed to be aimed at him. After he had been to church a second time Tom went round to the house and Bill was expecting him. He said, 'I was on my knees at three this morning praying to God to have mercy on my soul. Come and tell me how to get right with Him.' Tom led Bill and his wife Ivy to the Lord that night. What a stir it caused. His conversion was a fact the village could not gainsay. Bill had a week's holiday before the mission, and spent it visiting the five local public houses, inviting customers to come. When he won a boy for Christ, he was so excited he dashed home to his wife, and said, 'Ivy, quick, I've led a lad to the Lord. I'm going to buy you a new hat!'

Arthur disliked Tom at sight. People often did. He used to sit glowering at the back while Tom preached. He hated it, and gave life-like imitations of Tom afterwards, but he still had to come.

A year or so ago Tom said to me when we were motoring in the West Country, I must go round by Bridgwater. I have a girl friend there. The girl friend was just over a hundred, but she held Tom's hand and repeated with him, 'He that dwelleth in the secret place of the most High shall abide under the shadow of the Almighty.' This saint of God, years before, had given Arthur a birthday present. She always did. It was a good book, and a pound note. There was a note with the pound saying, 'My Spirit shall not always strive with man', and urging Arthur not to fight, but to become a Christian. He did. It was very humbling for him to tell Tom the next Sunday, 'I've become a Christian.' Immediately Tom invited Arthur to tell the people. With great courage he did. He was as exuberant as Tom had been. At our house, managing to eat between 'hallelujahs', Tom asked him to lead in prayer. With no hesitation Arthur prayed, 'O Lord, I do thank you for saving me. And Lord, these Rees's, you know how I used to hate them, but now Lord, I think they're damn fine people.'

With people praying in every lane and street there was a strong sense of the Lord's presence. Tom visited homes and was welcomed by 'Come in Mr. Rees, I was expecting you. I want to become a Christian.'

During the time of preparation, Tom was taking a meeting at Cheddar, where he was to have special services. He urged them to invite strangers to come. While he was speaking, three miles away in our own village a soldier was walking up the road on the way to Cheddar. As he went through the village where prayer was being made, and Christians were adjusting their lives to God, he had a strong conviction of sin. He thought of the days when he was a boy, and used to go to Salvation Army meetings. He longed to have someone to help him, and his soul cried out to God. Coming home from the meeting at Cheddar where Tom had been speaking was a mother and daughter. They passed the soldier, and the daughter said: 'I wish I'd invited that soldier to come tomorrow night like Mr. Rees told us to.' 'Go back and ask him,' said her mother. So the girl ran back and invited the soldier to come. The next night he came, and from the opening hymn he sat and wept. At the end Tom pointed him to Christ. He gave his testimony at a later meeting.

We had a great mission, and the work continued, Tom not only evangelising, but teaching.

In his diary on March 17th Tom spoke on the sin we are afraid to mention. This, it appears, is failing to give the Lord

His tithe. Again we were living by faith, and a bit of what Paul calls tent-making. The church was only able to promise us one pound a week for expenses, and this was an act of faith on their part, as their collections had rarely been more than five shillings a week. Tom planned to leave the church able to support a successor. So, like Paul, we made our tents; this took the form of buying old cottages and renovating them, and for two years this augmented our income. We never seemed short; we kept hens and grew tomatoes and vegetables.

It is strange that these happiest of days had the background of war. We were on the direct line to Bristol for enemy planes who, if they were disheartened, off-loaded their bombs to save them the full journey. It was when we were sitting happily in the garden, after a game of croquet with Roy Cattell, that we saw a plane with large black crosses dropping out little black things, missing us by one field. One lady of eighty felt quite deprived at missing the Bristol raids, and wanted to join her daughter there for a weekend, but she was quite satisfied when we had a stick of bombs in our High Street, killing five people.

We experienced tremendous love and tremendous opposition. Some would have almost laid down their lives for Tom, while others were convinced he was a spy, and spread appalling rumours about our showing lights to guide the enemy to bomb the secret sugar store!

We had time to talk and plan. Two subjects came out in conversation during our Mondays off, as we walked to Wells via Cheddar Gorge, or along the Mendips to Crook Peak. We wanted to start a conference centre like the Pinebrook which Tom had seen in the States, and Tom wanted to have the London evangelistic mission.

I had another desire, to which Tom was supremely indifferent. When we were first married, not only was aggressive evangelism out because of my health, but so was a baby. I suppose Tom had so many spiritual children that his parental instincts were satisfied, and he was so completely happy with me that he wanted nothing more; but I wanted a child with all my heart. When we had the green light from the doctor, it was still two full years before my prayer was answered.

I have read in books of the moment when 'she' whispers to 'him' the NEWS, and how he gently puts his arm around her. We had been talking about his coming mission in Lurgan. I took a deep breath and told him my NEWS—silence, and then Tom said, 'O well, I suppose it had to happen some time.' No happy discussion about names, and when, and where shall we buy the pram, but, 'As I was saying, I think at Lurgan I should talk to Christians first.'

In his diary I can read a few terse comments during the following week or so, such choice titbits as: 'Japan and U.S. are now at war. Peter Letchford broke out in chicken pox spots while playing at Service this morning.'

Nothing about me. No, I'm wrong—here it is:

'Jean is producing hundreds'—turn over the page—anticlimax—'producing hundreds of jam tarts and apple slices for the Forces Canteen.'

I must have overdone it, I imagine, for the next terse comment is: 'Jean had a miscarriage.'

I wonder if he ever understood the agony of disappointment with which I put the comment in the margin of my Bible at Psalm 37. I had ecstatically entered beside 'The Lord shall give thee the desires of thine heart' the date in November, and then later I added, 'In Thine own time, Lord.'

Tom went off the following February to Lurgan, his second mission in that Irish town. On his return my mother and I met him on the night train at Dumfries, and we travelling back to London together. He told us of the conversions; about how Heather Brown (later Olford) had rededicated her gift of playing to the Lord. Mother and I both commented on the way his face shone, and I thought at the time, 'I'm glad my baby's father looks like that. It is an honour for me and "it" ', for 'it' by now was on the way, and I didn't even tell Tom. I let him ask himself why I had a passion for tinned grapefruit!

In 1941 Tom's preaching was subtly changing. He studied

more, and there was a great deal of historical background in each sermon. My father had told me: 'You can always see the difference between a man to whom God has given the gift of a teacher, and the gift of an evangelist. The teacher is not so much interested in his congregation as in his subject. An evangelist is more interested in the people to whom he is preaching. He preaches for a verdict.' I told Tom (a good wife should be profitable for reproof, correction, and instruction!), and said rather sadly, 'It's time you were moving on.'

Our wonderful three years in a settled ministry were soon to be over. Tom had spent months talking over evangelism with me, and realised that if he merely waited for an invitation to preach, he would go where he was wanted and not where he was needed. He must take the initiative and go where he was not invited. As a pilot scheme he successfully took the Colston Hall, Bristol, without either backing or committee.

While visiting Dublin Tom had a burning desire to hold a mission in that centre of Roman Catholicism. The obvious place was the Y.M.C.A., but Tom decided to book the Round Room of the Mansion House. This mission was to have about it the touch of revival, but the cost of such invasions into the infernal regions is great. During the preparation Tom was in the depths, not of despair, but of spiritual conflict, wrestling in prayer. I had lessons to learn as well as Tom. After many obstacles had been overcome, and Tom's permit had been refused twice, and then finally granted, he got to Dublin. Eire was a neutral country; Germany still had an Embassy there, and there were stringent security precautions.

When Tom arrived he sent me a telegram. He wished to let me know that he was covered with remorse, and still adored me. It was a pity he did not say so in a straightforward manner, but he evidently thought that by using a kind of pidgin English it would be less embarrassing. Nothing could have been more embarrassing. When I received the telegram COVERED WITH MORSE STILL ADORE YOU I was approached by the police about this message in code. What was this 'morse'? It was terribly embarrassing to explain that my husband was full of remorse, but still adored me!

I became used to the problem of the 'evangelistic season' as years went on. In one of my diaries I say, 'I am so lonely for Tom, my Tom, not the dedicated man who lives in the same house as I do!' Towards the end of the Albert Hall series I would hardly be able to bear it. It was far easier when he went right away for a mission.

Mr. F. N. Martin, our great friend and Vice-President of the Trust, writes:

I was at the first Hildenborough Hall in the autumn of 1946 when Tom was campaigning in the Royal Albert Hall. He was so burdened with all that this involved, and so preoccupied with the tremendous problems that it posed that he often passed me without seeing me, yet in the conference sessions he was relaxed, and even boyish. This made a great impression on those who observed him.

When the mission ended, it was like the sun coming out! There are bits I treasure now that I see his diary for the first time: 'Only five days more until I see Jean. How I thank God upon every remembrance of her. I thank God that she has been given back to me.' Again he says: 'Thank God for Jean— she is my greatest temporal blessing, and my spiritual one.'

CHAPTER EIGHT

Starting a Family

ON October 19th, 1941, Jennifer was born. In war time it was almost impossible to get a hospital bed, so I had the baby at my parents' home in London. We had a very strong-minded nurse who disliked men in general, and Tom in particular on account of his religion. She was eaten up with superstition, and he enraged her by bringing me red and white flowers! Tom rescued the offending offering from the dustbin. The nurse retaliated by calling him 'Daddy', and told my parents that it was criminal the way her patient was depressed when 'Daddy' read aloud the sermons of a preacher called 'Sturgeon'!

On the day of Jennifer's arrival she told Tom he had better go out, they didn't want him under their feet. (When Jennifer, twenty-four years later, was having her baby, 'Daddy' was given a place of honour, allowed to be there, and great happiness prevailed.) When Tom returned home it was all over.

He was greeted: 'You've got a daughter, no thanks to you. Your wife had a heart failure; we needed oxygen, and you weren't there to make yourself useful!'

Tom comments in the diary: 'We nearly lost Jean. Thank God for His goodness. May the Lord save "it's" soul at an early age, and may it grow up to be an effective Christian—Amen.' He continues: 'The thought of this baby has depressed me beyond measure, particularly the last ten days. In fact I must

74

confess it has made me not a little bad tempered and irritable. Dear Lord, forgive me. The thought of a screaming infant, mess, the endless worry of it day and night has for a long time worried me. The Scripture teaches us that children are a blessing, but I must confess I fail to see how this can be, although it must be so. I can only see a child as a thing sent to try me. May the Lord teach me by experience that I am wrong.'

Over the years the Lord answered his fervent prayer. Before we had children he talked firmly about not sparing the rod, so I expected a harsh father who believed in corporal punishment, but only once did he chastise his son, and that very mildly. He confided in me he felt ill for days. 'Imagine a grown man hitting a child, especially his son. There must be a better way,' he said.

Fairly recently we were having Sunday lunch together and heard of a family who had thrown over their parents' teaching. Justyn was about to go off evangelising with his guitar, and Jen was going too, to sing. Tom asked, 'Why didn't you two go off at a tangent? It can't have been easy being brought up in a conference centre.'

'You never tried to be a good father,' they both explained to Tom, 'That is, you just took it for granted that we'd go the right way without giving us improving talks.' Our prayers must have helped, but Jen explained afterwards that 'the Boss' (we rarely called him anything else) was so lovely to go out with. 'Even when I was a little girl, he treated me like a very important lady, and took me to a good restaurant, and let me choose the menus as if I really mattered. He never talked down to me.'

When she was five Tom said all the books talked about 'mothering' times, so he was going to have a 'fathering' time each day after lunch. He read aloud to Jennifer out of a children's *Pilgrim's Progress*, and explained that Hildenborough Hall was 'House Beautiful' and our job was to help the pilgrims on their way to the Celestial City. Jennifer understood and revelled in the idea of the Albert Hall being the place where her father fought the battle. They had a special 'fathering' drawer which I have just found. In it was a poem Jennifer composed for Tom when she was eleven. It shows her insight into the spiritual fight.

> The Albert Hall stands big and bright,
> Beautiful music is played every night,
> But no! not today, haven't you heard?
> Tom Rees has come here to fight.

> But tell me, who is he going to fight?
> And what weapons will he use?
> The devil he'll fight with the weapon of prayer,
> And this is no new fangled ruse.

> Tom Rees has filled this massive Hall
> Over fifty times,
> And every night fights the fight of faith,
> And the choir sing out like golden chimes,
> And heavenward they rise.

It was a very proud father at an Easter Albert Hall rally who got his ten-year-old daughter to recite her own poem.

> Jesus rode upon an ass,
> And heard the people shout,
> The High Priests in the Temple,
> Planned to get the Saviour out.

> Along came Judas Iscariot,
> And said he had a plan,
> How he would kiss his Master,
> And they would take the Man.

And so He died upon the Cross,
To save the sins of men,
That one day they might go to Him,
And live in glory then.

And once again this Easter time,
I'm glad He died for me,
Although I'm only ten years old,
I know He's set me free.

With the years their friendship deepened. He taught her to learn the Bible by heart. When she could recite St. Luke's Gospel 'without book', Tom gave her a golf club—a number 8 iron.

I think every man hates losing his daughter to another man. At first Tom was very doubtful as to whether Tony was the right man for her. He wrote to Jennifer telling her to be quite sure, marriage was a very big step. I had no doubts. I had known Tony since he was in my choir as an enthusiastic sixteen-year-old, and I reminded Tom he was just like his father.

At a wedding speech, when one of my sisters was married, father told us: 'Someone asked me what are your sons-in-law like, and I said, they are excellent, splendid, satisfactory men, and I hate the lot of them!'

Jennifer brought light and joy when we were weighed down with anxiety and worry. On a holiday she brought a sparkle that was wonderful for both of us.

Tom was big enough to admit he was wrong about Tony. On the second anniversary of her wedding he wrote to her saying he had been quite mistaken; Tony was the very one for her, and he rejoiced that they were so happy. In the last few Hildenborough summers his organising help with the conferences and prayer support made for very happy fellowship.

It was a great joy to Jennifer and Tom to be alone together. They had long talks, and Jennifer confided in him. Tom's greatest relaxation was his stereophonic record player, and he loved listening with her to their favourites.

When Jennifer was with us in Florida I was writing a book called *Madame Estelle* and read a chapter each evening to entertain them.

'I think Mummy's very clever to write a book,' Jennifer said.

Tom, who had just finished his book *The Spirit of Life* said, 'I've written a book. Don't you think I'm clever?' To which Jennifer replied, 'But you had God to help you in your book. Mummy does her books without any help from God at all!'

I find it hard to believe, as I look at the diary, that Tom ever wrote, 'I can only see a child as a thing sent to try me.' Years later he wrote to Jennifer, 'The gift of you from God has given me the greatest possible joy.'

Jennifer, like Tom, did not dream very often, but the day before what would have been his fifty-ninth birthday (only three weeks after he died) she had a dream. Ruth Graham (Billy's wife) is convinced that those who die in Christ continue to work for us by their prayers. Don't let us have a doctrinal argument about this, but Jennifer had difficulty in bringing herself to believe that Tom was consciously with the Lord and intelligibly knowing joy in heaven. The day before his birthday she said: 'I saw him in a dream, full of vigour, wearing his brown suit. He said to me, "I do want you to realise how wonderful heaven is. Don't forget, the more you learn about the Lord on earth, the more wonderful it is here." In the dream he quoted the lines of a couplet:

Only one life, 'twill soon be past,
Only what's done for Jesus will last.'

She woke up, feeling her father had sent her a special message. She said nothing to Tony of her dream, but at tea time he said, 'It's strange, but I've had two lines of a hymn ringing in my ear all day. Do you know them? "Only one life, 'twill soon be past ..."'

A few days later, at Tom's memorial service, Prebendary Maurice Wood—now Bishop of Norwich—told the congregation that Tom had written specific instructions about the service ten years before he died.

'If my relations desire a memorial service,' he wrote, 'it should be a really cheerful occasion with good hymn singing, and a stirring word of exhortation, calling on Christian people to remember:

Only one life, 'twill soon be past,
Only what's done for Jesus will last.'

CHAPTER NINE

Planning Ahead

TOM did not like to spoil a walk by stopping to hit a little white ball, but he loved walking. All our best plans were made when, stick in hand, and haversacks on our backs, we started off on a long trek. Having decided that an evangelist should 'stir up the gift that is within him', we went for a break to Scotland and set off for a walking tour from Newton Stewart beside the River Cree.

Tom loved to talk over propositions, 'to-ing and fro-ing' he called it, and I had to learn not to be too enthusiastic or run ahead.

There were two big items on our agenda, as we walked through unbelievably lovely country. We wanted to open a conference centre like the one called Pinebrook in the States, the British version of which would be an English mansion, a stately home. We reasoned they would be two a penny after the war was finished, when the Army relinquished occupation, but Tom was never content to have one idea, and with the urge to start the conference centre was a burning desire to have a big evangelistic crusade in London.

We talked ourselves hoarse, Tom emphasising each point with a thump on his walking stick, then realised it was time we found somewhere to sleep. It was getting late, about nine o'clock, when we found a little Inn called 'Top of the Hill'. The owner was very sorry there was no room available unless

At Hildenborough Hall, Roy Cattel, Mr. and Mrs. Montague Goodman,
Sir William and Lady Dobbie, Jean, and Tom Rees.

Bringing up children in a Conference Centre
was not easy.

Tom with his three Jays, Jennifer, Justyn,
and Jean.

An Evangelist with no tricks or appeal to mass hysteria; 'Sing it London' in the Central Hall, Westminster, with Lady Bates, Roy Cattel, Tony Groom, and Branse Burbridge.

we were willing to go to bed after ten o'clock. We were willing, and soon after ten we were given our candle, and shown into an extraordinary bedroom containing a large double bed, and a sideboard with levers, the whole having a peculiar smell. When it was light we discovered we had been sleeping in the bar!

During the next months we experienced disappointment upon disappointment. After a series of missions all over Ulster called Victory Crusades, to Tom's intense excitement he booked the Christian Youth Holiday Camp at Careagh in Downpatrick, when he and I were going to organise a holiday conference for 500 young people, including many new converts. The experience, of course, would be invaluable to us in planning our own conference centre. Then the Government commandeered the premises and everything had to be cancelled.

It was when Tom was in Ireland that he received a telegram from Mr. Lindsay Glegg (whom Tom at nineteen had considered 'the sanest Christian he had ever met') inviting him to join a team of evangelists to speak in the Royal Albert Hall under the title 'Faith for the Times'. Tom was very interested, and wondered if this was the answer to his prophecy, made when he was only seventeen, to his friend Eric Wells. The Rev. Eric Wells, now a vicar in Bognor, wrote and reminded me recently that Tom had told him, 'One day I will preach to thousands of people in the Royal Albert Hall.' Eric Wells said this was not boastfully spoken. 'I can only liken it to the way in which the great maritime explorers as boys sat on the shore gazing over the sea and determining that one day the Voice that calls so insistently will be answered by them. Tom answered the Voice that called; in fact, he was answering that Voice all his life.'

Mr. Glegg was a modern Barnabas; a man who, although very gifted himself, was big enough to 'bring on' young men. Tom came to London as the youngest member of the team, and was delighted to have the opportunity of preaching in this national auditorium. This week of meetings deepened the desire he had for a prolonged London mission. He asked the committee if they would consider joining him in a month's crusade in the Central Hall Westminster, but Tom soon learned that committees rarely feel the time is ripe, or have a sense of urgency. 'Faith for the Times' was Mr. Glegg's vision, and although with his gracious manner he appeared to be arranging things with the committee, it was no doubt his vision that was the driving force.

Tom decided to go it alone. Together we went to the offices of the Central Hall, Westminster, and asked if we could book the hall for four weeks in September 1944. The secretary was delighted; there were no bookings; central London was deserted. He asked what organisation Tom represented, and could he give them a cheque for £300 as a deposit. Tom explained that he didn't represent anyone, and after a whispered colloquy, we found we could do the £300 by putting in our life savings. We didn't have the slightest anxiety about the rightness of the whole idea; we just knew it was God's will for us.

Tom formed—I won't call it a committee—but a small group of like-minded young men to work with him: Roy Cattell, now a Canon in Northamptonshire; Gordon Glegg, the gifted scientist, son of Lindsay Glegg; and Geoffrey Lester, now Prebendary of Bath Abbey. The plans went full steam ahead. At last Tom could get his teeth into the thing he had dreamed since the vision in his teens. The diary bristles with activity.

On April 25th, 1944, immediately after the 'Faith for the Times' he writes: 'Travelled up to Liverpool. Jean typed letters for me all the way on the portable. Saw the Royal Philharmonic Hall—a good place for a mission.' (He booked it a few months later.)

Through May the diary is alive with purposeful work: 'Designed prayer cards, designed notepaper. We have chosen "This is the victory" as our slogan. Planned stewarding. Wrote to well-known men as supporters. Spent all the morning writing letters, Jean helping me. Roy Cattell came in and we worked all the evening, planning with Geoffrey Lester and Gordon Glegg.'

The flying bomb attack paralysed large scale activity in London, and on July 7th Tom spent a depressed day: 'Spent the day in gloom over the whole situation. Guide me, Lord. We decided to postpone the Central Hall, Westminster campaign. This is the first day of the postponed Irish Camp.'

It is the complete hiatus that is so hard to take when you are full of zeal and desire to serve the Lord. But back to Joseph and his years of waiting. It is the waiting that builds character. On July 11th Tom writes from the depths of his Welsh soul: 'Spent the day writing about the postponement. Feeling in the depths of gloom.' July 13: 'Spent a day of gloom. Jean and I walked at 5 p.m. and I became a little cheered.'

We had to reorganise our lives. We had sold our Banwell house and made plans to move to London. Now we went to Scotland, and due to the kindness of my brother, Colin, were able to occupy temporarily one of his farmhouses.

We were in a strange vacuum. It is one thing, when one is exhausted and overworked, to find a haven of rest, but we were not like that. With all the pent up energy of several years of praying and preparing we were ready to be expended in unstinting work, using mind, body, and soul.

From the depths of gloom Tom became calm. The Lord gave him peace about the next few months. He said to me: 'I believe this is the last time I will ever be really quiet and have a chance to study and revise my sermons.' He buried himself in a little study and revised, annotated, and prepared all the sermons God had given him in Banwell and the years before. He also wrote his first book *His Touch has still its Ancient Power*, exciting stories of conversions. He urged me into writing, and I wrote the first of my children's stories. I never thought that it would start me off on a career of well over thirty books. But those quiet months in 1944 and 1945 gave us our chance. Tom writes in November: 'I have had some very happy times in prayer and during this time I have been very happy in my soul. I wonder when we will learn that God knows best about timing?'

Our second great desire was to open the conference centre, a place for training in Christian leadership and evangelism, where holidays could be invested and not spent. Had we held the Central Hall campaign in 1944 we would have had no time to search for the premises, or plan for what came to be Tom's life work.

While flying bombs were still roaring over London, Tom and I set off to look for what we called 'the mansion'. Tom wasn't the only one who had disappointments; I had hoped there would have been a brother for Jennifer on the way, but although there is no mention of it in Tom's diary, I was recovering from another miscarriage.

Our search was rewarded, and in Kent, in the village of Hildenborough, we found the premises that we knew was 'IT'.

Tom's father retired from business early that year. He had stayed with us in Banwell and proved a delightful companion, but could not make head or tail of Tom's way of life. When he came home from an Irish mission, quite exhausted, Pop would say, 'Well, you don't look much better for your holiday.' Holiday! Tom didn't explain.

When Tom found the conference centre of his choice, he suddenly decided to tell his father about the scheme. To Tom's astonishment he offered to lend the initial capital to purchase the house. When I told Pop how much we appreciated it, he said: 'Trust old Tom. I would lend him anything, safe as the Bank of England.'

We asked various people for advice, confidentially, but although we did not know it, my father had got wind of the scheme. He was a man of great business ability, and Tom and I felt pleased that we only needed to ask for his advice, not for his financial help at this stage. One of his rather irritating sayings was, 'The Lord will provide, but it's really only father!' We invited father to tea in the farmhouse we were occupying in Scotland.

Have you ever seen a business man, who knows he is going to be asked to help in a financial way? He's probably going to give in, but walks warily, determined to play hard to get. We thought father knew nothing of our enterprise, and he listened with rather heavy breathing, puffing a bit, looking cautiously round. Of course, Tom and I were totally inexperienced, and part of father's plan of attack was to discredit us if he could, in a kindly way.

'Making a pessimistic estimate . . .?' Tom said.

Father grunted, 'Conservative estimate—you don't even know the *terms*.'

Tom came to the end of his story and paused. Father breathed heavily again, waited, and then said, 'All right, break it gently, how much do you want to borrow?'

'Nothing,' said Tom. 'We only want your moral support and prayer. My father is going to lend us the money.'

Suddenly father became genial and expansive, gave us every kind of advice, arranged introductions about mortgages and other loans; told us if there was any way in which he could help, we had only to ask, and then heavily closed the proceedings with prayer. From then on he was immensely helpful and showed great appreciation in all our enterprises.

CHAPTER TEN

London Rallies

THE next year was one of new things. It brought peace in Europe in May, and we forged ahead with the September campaign, and discovered that our slogan, suggested by Geoffrey Lester, 'This is the Victory' was really appropriate. It certainly was an adventure. The way we worked with so little help reminds me of the story of an American Christian ringing up a British evangelist:

'Say, I'm interested in the work of your organisation, and how you do evangelism over here. I would like to meet your song leader, publicity man, follow-up chief, preparations secretary, finance expert. Could you arrange it?' The British evangelist replied: 'Come along, I'm right here.'

We had no large central offices, but the top flat of my parents' home in Bishop's Avenue, and an office ten feet square in which Heather Brown and I did the typing, Tom and Roy breezing in and out. We worked all our waking hours and many of our sleeping ones. All over London, in the tubes, outside churches, the poster 'This is the Victory' caught the eyes of Londoners.

Tom came to London as a new voice. The Rev. John T. Carson, who a year or so ago was the Moderator of the General Assembly of The Presbyterian Church in Ireland, commented: 'T. B. Rees is a young man, but his words are full of power. He is not so well known in his own country as he is in Ireland where his name is a household word.'

After the frustrations and disappointments; the stored nervous energy and spiritual power, preparation and discipline were all used for the next years of opportunity. Over the years on the battle grounds of Ulster, in Londonderry, Lurgan, Newtownards, Ballymena, Belfast, and Dublin, he had learnt not to be over-elated at success, or over-despondent at failure. When his Welsh temperament gave him depths of depression, he leaned harder on his Lord.

Before the campaign, while Roy, Heather, and I were handling printing crises, endless correspondence and the final preparation, Tom went to Sevenoaks to pray. He writes: 'Spent much time in the Parvis praying ... Next day from 10.30 to noon in the Parvis, and then in Knole Park during the afternoon. I had to hold on in faith that God was hearing me. Spent the rest of the week in prayer until August 29th.' When all was nearly ready: 'Jean came down for me in the car. We walked over "One Tree Hill" and had a good time in prayer.' Putting ten thousand to flight was our calling, and both of us were utterly abandoned for the spiritual attack.

If unborn children are affected by the prenatal state of their parents, it is no wonder Justyn has an evangelistic outlook. He was to be born four months later, but I was catering for a party of twenty in my parents' home, and devoting September to the campaign. Heather Brown and Roy were there and several others. We started in the early morning, and rarely were in bed the same day.

The Central Hall, Westminster was packed on the opening Saturday. Mr. Lindsay Glegg introduced Tom in his inimitable way as 'the atomic Tom', and Tom spoke convincingly on 'I am not ashamed of the Gospel'. I can hardly believe my eyes when I read Tom's comments: 'Went home thoroughly satisfied thanking God for His goodness.' It was very seldom he admitted any satisfaction after his preaching. It was a wonderful month. People queued for seats from four o'clock, and in order to accommodate the young people and members of the Forces, the ground floor was reserved for the under thirties. Militant old ladies fought for seats with umbrellas, causing many of the stewards to think that the war was not yet over! Some wonderful men who are now with the Lord were guest speakers— General Sir William Dobbie and Dr. W. E. Sangster. C. S. Lewis told us, 'Everything must begin with conversion. If there were to be a substantial majority of truly converted Christians, it would make all the difference in world affairs, for the really converted Christian is irresistible.'

Gipsy Smith, that great evangelist of the early part of this century, was heard for the last time publicly at our closing meeting. For this Tom had rented the Royal Albert Hall, and could have filled it several times over. There were as many outside as inside, and the service was relayed, although Tom did go outside to say a word to the assembled throng. With the minimum of advertising, organisation and expense (the month's campaign cost less than £3,000) thousands came and thousands found Christ.

This was the beginning of the fulfilment of Tom's prophecy concerning the Royal Albert Hall, although he did not choose this as a venue for his subsequent evangelism. As an auditorium for evangelism it is a most difficult place, but it has a fascination, with the Royal Box, and its association with national events.

Tom hoped to have had rallies in the Central Hall, Westminster the following winter, and booked it from February to Easter, but the Government commandeered it for a UNO Conference. They may have taken Tom's holiday camp from under his nose, but he wasn't lying down under this, so he booked the Royal Albert Hall for the corresponding Saturdays, and sent the bill for the extra rent and advertising to the Government. After an argument, to our astonishment they sent a cheque.

This was the beginning of nearly ten years' evangelism with the Royal Albert Hall as the high spot. Tom called this famous auditorium 'My little mission hall in Kensington' and those who attended the rallies will never forget the thrill when he stepped to the microphone, and said: 'Good evening, Everyone.'

It is difficult to express the tremendous effect of Tom's consecrated personality on the platform, although I was with him on all but one of the fifty-five occasions (you must be allowed ten days off to have a baby!). On February 2nd Roy Cattell announced that Tom had a son and heir, and a few days later I was there, and Tom called upon me to sing a duet with him.

He could make the thousands of people in the Royal Albert Hall sound like a trained choir. One bishop, impressed with Tom's gifts and ability, fell into Mr. Langston's trap. 'I would like to ordain you,' he said. 'I am sure this is all you need at this point of your career to ensure complete success.'

Tom, now having more wisdom, did not mention baptismal regeneration, but explained that he felt he would be more useful as an interdenominational preacher. The bishop was incensed, and advised Tom to cut out hymns that mentioned the blood of Christ 'and that chorus you had "There's a wonder-working power in the blood of Calvary". Out of date,' he said. Apparently hell has no fury like a bishop scorned. Princess Elizabeth and Princess Margaret were to attend the next rally. The Royal Box was prepared, but a letter to the Palace arrived from our friend, the incensed bishop, suggesting there would be items in the Royal Albert Hall rally that might offend the sensitive young minds of the Princesses, and it would be wiser if they did not attend. The visit was cancelled.

When Tom was unleashed on London he took it by storm. Whereas in our preparation it was difficult to get a few lines in the cautious Christian press, after the September campaign pages were devoted to it, and in subsequent years they were hungry for any information Tom had to give.

Other campaigns followed, in such cities as Newcastle, Glasgow, Liverpool, but London was peculiarly Tom's parish, and the 'little mission hall in Kensington' was his centre. Few people have been able to evangelise in London continuously, although there have been big missions from time to time, but for nearly ten years Tom maintained the confidence of his public. Lloyd George once commented: 'You need take no notice of a man until he is able to fill the Royal Albert Hall.'

Although Tom had a wonderful team of gifted helpers and supporters, he was in everything, and I suppose as he and I worked together so much, it gave us a close touch with the nerve centre.

Here we are planning the following season while going on a holiday to Scotland, travelling overnight because it is better for the children. They are bedded down in the back of the car, but for us there is hot coffee in a thermos and a shorthand notebook in my hand. 'Let's have different nights,' Tom said. 'We'll have a Sports' Night, a Medical Night, a Toughs' Night ...' If I flagged, Tom said, 'Have some more coffee; you mustn't get sleepy, or I will.' It was a ten-hour and four-hundred-mile committee meeting. On one Sports' Night, which coincided with the Boat Race, Gordon Glegg, with a fast car and police co-operation, swooped on a Christian man from the winning Cambridge boat, and brought him to give his testimony amid loud cheers.

We had a choir of about three hundred voices, which I led. It was not the kind of choir which 'rendered items'. The singers knew that their job was to be a prayer force; Tom told them they were soldiers as well as singers. We had many hilarious moments. Tom, running through the programme with them said, 'The collection—and then it's "Mine! Mine! Mine!"' Practising the hymn 'Sound the battle cry', I said, 'Beginning of the last verse, girls only, and then the men come in "When the battle's done, and the victory won".'

People arrived in their coach parties to find an air of festivity at the Royal Albert Hall. It was for everyone; the aristocrats in the boxes, the parties in the arena, the late-comers thronging the top standing gallery. The rallies had ceased to become a spiritual picnic after a series or two, and churches, Bible classes, and individuals used them for evangelism.

In 1950 we introduced the Gideonite Prayer Fellowship which changed the whole spiritual temperature. Hundreds of people were converted before the series started because Christian people started praying, realising that the rallies were ideally the labour ward for spiritual births, rather than the first contact. For nearly two hours Tom held his audience spellbound. If he felt the pace was dragging, he used some impromptu item to regain attention; some exalted person from the platform was invited to sing a duet with him, or answer a question.

Here is a quote from a reporter who was asked to write an article on 'Is London Pagan or Christian?' After visiting St. Paul's Cathedral and various other churches, he was advised to attend an Albert Hall rally. He wrote: 'Tom B. Rees is a master of mass psychology. It was clear that he knew the technique of preaching, and was also aware of the art of the actor, but it must be said there was nothing cheap-jackish or quack-doctorish with his methods. He was aflame with his message of conversion and salvation. He declared that religion was meant to be a dynamic, not a soporific. I heard Mr. Rees speak on three occasions. He reached a high standard of doctrinal learning and persuasive oratory, while he carefully released tension by the judicious use of humour. He emphasised incessantly the necessity of squaring daily life with the Christian profession. At the Royal Albert Hall every one of the ten thousand seats was occupied, and outside hundreds clamoured vainly for admission.'

Here is a comment from *The Star* on March 11th, headed 'Orator Without Tricks'. 'There is a man of thirty-four who can fill the Royal Albert Hall six Saturdays running. He is an evangelist with no tricks of the top orator, or the appeal to mass hysteria. This is Thomas B. Rees who has a good, though untrained, voice. He has never learned music, but he is a master at getting crowds to sing. He conducts all the services himself.'

In dozens of reports in both Christian and secular magazines there is an appreciation of 'evangelism without tricks'. These had brought evangelism into disrepute. Tom's great fear during the whole of his evangelistic ministry was that evangelism should be degraded. When, after nearly ten years of evangelism in central London, the way was paved for Billy Graham's massive Crusade, Tom said to me, 'How I thank God for Billy's message—"What the Bible says"—without distortion or deviation, and his straightforward method of calling people to commitment.'

Tom's preaching changed over the years. At first he constantly told Bible stories, becoming the person whose story he was telling—David, trying on Saul's armour—and on one never-to-be-forgotten occasion in the Central Hall, Westminster, he was both Jonathan and his armour bearer. King Saul was sitting under a pomegranate tree, imaginary pomegranate in hand, eating vulgarly and spitting out the pips. We got a letter a day or so later from an old lady complaining of Tom's coarse behaviour, and saying that one of the pips had actually hit her on the front row!

In a talk on Eliezer seeking a wife for Isaac, each character came to life. Laban, the surly brother, hearing about the unexpected visitor—'What does he think we are, a hotel?' But 'When he saw the earring Rebekah had been given—"Come in, thou blessed of the Lord; wherefore standest thou without?"' The climax came when Rebekah was asked, 'Wilt thou go with this man? And she said, I will go.'

Lindsay Glegg recalls:

I think in the early days Tom built up his reputation because he had scriptural truths right in his heart. He loved the Word of God, and he could quote it most effectively from memory, but then he had the power of illustration. Everyone was struck with that when he first came to the Royal Albert Hall. He could mimic a Chinaman to perfection, a Yorkshireman, or a Scotsman. As he developed he was so soaked in the Word of God that it was an exposition, and illustration was not called for, because we were being gripped by the Scriptures and the arguments of Scripture. His sense of humour was a great asset, and he could preach from the authority of God's Word and drive it home. I last heard him on the Deity of Christ, an amazing hour's worth, in which there was not a sentence that did not hold something that was bearing on the subject. He built up a tremendous case by Scripture, not by the authority of quoting other people, or by any other argument. Tom knew his message—he had been through it on his knees before God, and then he came out to the people as a prophet. I had tears in my eyes when I listened to Tom's message because it so exalted the Lord.

CHAPTER ELEVEN

Hildenborough

IN 1945 we started twenty-five years' hard labour. On our tour amid the flying bombs we found the mansion we wanted, and from then every minute of our time, every bit of our brains, ingenuity, and executive ability was needed to prepare the conference centre to be called Hildenborough Hall. Miracles happened all the time. It seems absurd to have bought a house with over thirty acres for £6,000, but when the Government gave us £2,000 bomb damage, because of a little accident at the greenhouse with a German Messerschmidt, and the training college officials, who had recently occupied the house, sent another £2,000 for dilapidations, we set about with a will to do what was almost the impossible; buy furniture, linen and equipment.

We moved in on November 5th and were wonderfully blessed in Miss Frances Hay, coming all the way from County Donegal to be manageress. She possessed executive ability, a capacity for hard work, and a tremendous sense of humour. Elizabeth Smith, from Glasgow, started as assistant cashier, but was to become cashier, organiser, and finally secretary of the Hildenborough Evangelistic Trust. Joyce Silcox came—she was the girl of fourteen converted in the cinema service at Seaford, and she and I are retracing the road together as we do this biography. With Heather Brown, Tom's secretary and pianist, we took on a task that appalls us now.

When we had all worked very hard, Heather and I (a kind of

female trade union) asked about a day off, or even half a day. Tom and Roy looked at us. 'Day off!' said Tom. 'Day *off*?' asked Roy. We murmured something about getting our hair done and shopping, and said we had been working until very late each evening. Miss Hay in her astringent way assured us that it wasn't late until midnight, and after that it was early! Of course, we got ourselves better organised later. When Joyce joined us, fresh from the Sun Insurance Company, she kept telling us that 'in a proper office . . . things are done differently'. Ours was a pioneer effort, and Heather and I were a bit amateurish as office workers, I was seven months pregnant, and Heather's shorthand was more long than short, but her glorious piano playing more than made up for it, and charmed Tom's savage breast, or soothed his worried mind.

In January 1946 I went to the Middlesex Hospital where Justyn was born. No heart failure this time, and when I rang Tom up and told him he'd had a son twenty minutes ago, his relief was immense. He wrote: 'This evening Jean phoned to tell me the good news that Justyn Hereward Sinclair Rees had arrived. Lord, take this child, save, bless, and use him for Christ's sake—Amen.'

I read in my Scripture portion that night about John the Baptist being 'great in the sight of the Lord', and earnestly prayed that this would be Justyn's experience.

With all the work and preparation for the conference centre, it was wonderful to have such a good baby. Tom never heard him cry until he was three months old. No one could say that because he was called Hereward after his great-grandmother, it was because he was 'the Wake'!

We had embarked on what was one of the most rewarding enterprises of twenty-five years. We never lost the thrill of a party arriving, with all its spiritual potential.

The house, approached by an avenue of Canadian redwoods, stood well, and after a coat of Snowcem, looked superb. By the side of lawns sloping down to the lake was a waterfall and stream with Cumberland rock, and rare trees and plants were interspersed with the glory of the spring azaleas and summer roses.

In those days the season started at Easter, and did not finish until October, and before that the winter evangelistic programme of Saturday activities had started, so we were stretched to the utmost. Tom was vitally concerned over every conference. If by Wednesday during the week he did not feel we were getting anywhere, he called us together for special prayer. By 'getting nowhere' I do not mean any special emotional excitement or crisis, but Tom felt that each person should go away transformed, encouraged, inspired—many with new life. Each conference was a milestone. No special blessings or short cuts to holiness were tolerated, but Tom wanted our guests to learn to pray and study the Bible, and to go away realising that Christianity was a responsibility—they were 'saved to serve'.

The guests arrived at tea time on Saturday and stayed until after breakfast the following Saturday, and then with a hectic physical and mental change, we prepared for the new party to arrive that same day for tea. The week was packed with fun, games, tournaments, and excursions, but the main attractions, believe it or not, were the two sessions, a thought-provoking Bible talk after breakfast, and an informal discussion, question session, or talk at night. The programme was geared for Christian people, but hardly a week passed without someone finding new life in Christ. Occasionally they survived the ordeal apparently unscathed, only to find that Christ had invaded their lives later. One such was Eddy Vann. He was a boxer, an enormous man brought by a diminutive girl friend who was sad that he boasted at the end of the week he had 'stood up for seven rounds at Hildenborough without a knock-out', but the very next week in a simple service the message got under his guard, and Eddy became a Christian. I can remember well his coming to the Royal Albert Hall to speak. On a previous occasion he had won a boxing match there in the arena, and speaking of his conversion he emphasised each point by a left hook!

Another guest, an army officer, who apparently survived the attack without giving in, was the father of a Hildenborough

Billy Graham's first day in Britain, staying at Hildenborough Hall with Charles Templeton, Stratton Schufelt, and Torrey Johnson.

'You need take no notice of any man until he can fill the Royal Albert Hall.'
—Lloyd George.

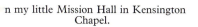

n my little Mission Hall in Kensington Chapel.

There were as many people outside the Albert Hall as inside. The service was relayed.

Fifty-five times, with the slogan 'Get right with God'.

teenage convert. This young man, having found Christ, determined to win his parents. He gave his mother a Homemakers' weekend conference as a birthday present, and that was successful, so the Major was then target number one. Like Eddy he survived the first onslaught, but at a rally in the Royal Albert Hall was attacked in the flank, and what a Christian home they have made.

Miss Hay and I often chatted concerning the conference season, saying one season was like a lifetime. In the spring we were thrilled and excited to start again, and felt about twenty-five. We felt a bit middle-aged by August, but got a second wind, and although we were able to live in the present, feeling each conference had a separate entity, by the end of the season we felt well over seventy, and were so mentally spent that we would have given the centre away gladly to anyone who would take it on. Tom indiscreetly said at a family lunch, 'I am so tired, I could almost hope for a fire—after all, we're insured.' Little Jennifer explained to the staff later that if the Hall caught fire, they weren't to put it out because Daddy wanted the 'assurance' money!

We owed much to our speakers who came with power and rich ministry. Tom's brother, Dick, was an outstanding help. In serving spiritual food he was like a chef who took infinite pains, the spiritual garnish and extras were there in good measure. Everyone was given duplicated notes. Dick often took over for the week, giving Tom a much needed rest.

The conferences with Stephen Olford were exceptional. His outstanding gift at a conference was for personal interviews, and he gave himself totally to the task.

Two leading younger men who came first as assistant hosts, and then graduated to speaker status, like Stephen Olford, found their wives at Hildenborough Hall. 'You want the best wives, we have them' could have been said to the Rev. John Taylor, now Vice-Principal of Oak Hill Theological College. His wife, Linda, was converted as a teenager, and has certainly been God's gift to John. His rare teaching ability allied to first class scholarship has made him an asset in conference work. He has recently written a foreword to Tom's book *Can Intelligent People Believe?* He and Tom went to the same school, but John was certainly never the dud of the lower fourth!

Eric Alexander from Glasgow spent most of his vacations with us at Hildenborough in the early days, and those who have heard him at Keswick realise the tremendous gift that God has given him. We certainly are proud of the young man who came down wearing a kilt and graduated to wearing a clerical collar as an outstanding minister of the Church of Scotland. On one of our last journeys together Tom and I went to Scotland for a family wedding, and he preached in Eric's church, and we were entertained by his wife, Greta, whom he had met at Hildenborough.

I wish we could tell more about the power of Alan Redpath's conferences, the common sense of Godfrey Robinson, the pawky wit of Dr. Graham Scroggie, the deep conviction of Archdeacon Herbert Cragg.

After an exacting winter's evangelistic programme, by the next spring we were raring to go and felt twenty-five again, with the same appetite for punishment.

Tom was totally occupied with the conference and evangelistic work, every ounce of his energy and time was taken up. We did manage to have a day off on our tenth wedding anniversary, in the middle of the summer conference season, and went to Seaford and sat in the car on the front, when Tom fell fast asleep! I reminded myself our happiness was a bonus, and I could very easily degenerate into a 'I never *see* you'—'*When* are we going to go out together' type of wife. I decided if you can't beat them, join them, so I became the Conference Secretary at Hildenborough Hall, and with Elizabeth as my secretary, we undertook all the bookings. Gradually I took over the office organisation, and coped with Tom's letters, and found I could dictate a letter that sounded more like him than he did himself. I revelled in the work with Miss Hay; we knew all about everyone who was coming, and I was so busy that it did my heart good when Tom said, 'When are *you* going to be free to come out with me.' I graciously agreed to try to fit him in!

Tom, as well as preparing for an important meeting, would cope with a member of the staff who had a grievance, another who had trouble at home, or a spiritual problem, patiently advising and praying with each one. He would have a quick visit to Diggle, his old landlady, who was blind; check and approve printing proofs, decide about suspected dry rot in the lounge, find time for a hospital visit, carry an undercurrent of financial anxiety over accounts, yet be cheery and relaxed at dinner with the guests, telling them stories about Buttercup Joe. He would take a session, conducting singing, leading a discussion, and have several personal talks on urgent problems.

Between 1945 and 1948 his programme included city-wide missions, conferences, scarcely without a let-up. He almost ground to a halt. He wrote in his diary in 1948 : 'My only desire is to run away and be alone and sleep for weeks and weeks.' His old enemy insomnia attacked him constantly. 'Tried to sleep. Hopeless. Got up and walked in Knole Park until 3 a.m.' However, in November of that year he writes : 'The Lord has given me great happiness. I am free for the first time from depression for many months. I think the reason is I am cutting down next year's programme, and have had two weeks' holiday with Jean.'

I remember it well. We went to the South of France. The travel allowance was only £30, and we stayed in strange places. One was called The Bananarie, all in for a pound a day. We walked and talked.

'You've got to help me,' Tom said as we took a path above the Mediterranean on the way to Menton. 'I am not organising my prayer life properly, there is so much to do.' He besieged all his waking hours. 'I must do something,' he said, emphasising his point with his walking stick. 'I get to bed so late that I can't get up at six o'clock as I used to. For some reason I must have my eight hours' sleep if possible. I'm no John Wesley.' We planned that he should go to his study and be unavailable until ten o'clock. The early hours belonged to God, and only earth-quake, sudden death, or act of God must be allowed to interfere with this rule.

Our holidays were times of re-creation. Tom talked out his inhibitions, and we tried to 'take thought', but not 'anxious thought'. When we arrived at our hotel we rang for the lift. 'I'll shut the door,' said Tom, 'and you press the button—we'll be able to save some seconds.' We chose our meal at speed, and were first out of the dining room until it dawned upon us that there was no need to save seconds. Tom told me then, and on every holiday until 1970, 'I have ceased to become an effective evangelist. People used to get converted when I preached, but they don't now.' I always replied, 'You've been telling me that since you were twenty-four.' I would instance people who had recently become converted through his ministry and were forging ahead, and he would brighten up.

CHAPTER TWELVE

The Growing Children

I HAD a great longing to have a place of our own, a bolt hole, somewhere to go on our day off, where we could talk. For nearly ten years we had only a bedroom and a rather gloomy nursery with no real home life at all. I used to scour the country to find a small cottage, and like all husbands Tom would find wonderful reasons why it would not be suitable, so we did nothing until one day I found a house right outside the drive gates of the Hall. I imagined all our crates of wedding presents unpacked, a kitchen of my own—I couldn't wait to tell Tom.

He had been praying earnestly for a colleague. We knew that Tom needed help, and the person above everyone else he would have chosen was Oliver Styles, the young convert of Seal, who was considering joining us.

'I've got something marvellous to tell you,' I said to Tom, bursting to share about the house at the drive gates.

'I've got something to tell *you*,' he said.

'There's a house, "The Croft", right at the gates for sale.'

'Marvellous,' said Tom, 'a real answer to prayer. Oliver is going to join us. It will be the very house for him and his family.'

Unless Tom is reading this book from heaven, he will never know what a blow this was to me, but God is very wonderful, and I realised almost immediately that we had to be right on the spot and continue 'living over the shop', especially as I was so involved with the organisation.

But at this point the worm turned, and I stopped looking for cottages, and decided to act. We must have somewhere for a day off, to sleep and talk, and so I ordered a portable wooden cabin with a bedroom and sitting room—incredibly cheap by modern prices. We would put it up in the woods quite easily. Unfortunately I forgot to tell Tom I'd ordered it! It arrived at the tradesmen's entrance. 'What on earth is this?' Tom asked me. I was appalled. The only other occasion when I had acted independently was when I bought a hen house and twelve hens during the war.

'It's a portable cabin,' I said, 'a bolt hole for us.' Tom was big-minded, and accepted the situation. He chose the site and organised the construction, and never failed to tell me how clever I was to have bought it, and that it saved his sanity and spiritual life. It was, of course, inevitably nicknamed by the staff 'Uncle Tom's Cabin'. On our days off we could have the children with us on our own, and in times of insomnia Tom often slept there away from the pressure of work.

Bringing up a family at the conference centre was not easy. I did try to spend as much time as possible with the children, and each year, although Tom could not be spared, I took them to Scotland for a holiday, and Tom's father and mother often joined us.

We hired a small boat with an outboard motor to chug round the back of a little island in the Solway Firth. It was as exciting and hazardous to us as a trip round the back side of the moon! Pop and Lolo, Jennifer and Justyn and I were the passengers. Round the head the little boat behaved like a cockle shell, we all felt sick, and were very scared excepting schoolboy Justyn. 'I'm all right,' he told us. 'You may get drowned, but I'm quite safe.' When asked to explain, he told us cheerfully, 'God told Mummy when I was born that I would be great in the sight of the Lord, and you all know I'm not that yet.' I must have told Justyn at an early age the text that I had in my reading when he was born, and so he had that relaxed feeling that enabled Peter

102

in prison to sleep, and know that he would not be martyred in the morning because Jesus had said, 'When thou art old ... another will gird thee.'

Justyn was very independent. In our hectic life at the conference centre we managed to have lunch together each day. Father to Justyn was a rather mysterious figure who appeared from the study, either throwing him in the air, making animal noises, or being preoccupied according to the state of evangelism in general and the conference centre in particular. Tom was never bad tempered or irritable, but he was always a force to be reckoned with.

Justyn was like a bird born in captivity. Unlike Jennifer, who had known the joys of living in a small house that was home, Justyn had always lived in a conference centre, inhabited by strange, friendly adults called staff, and even stranger people called guests, who came and went, and had a tendency to produce cameras on sight and say, 'Ooh, let's take a photo of the little Reeses.' He soon learned to take evasive action, and the sight of guests arriving became the sign to vanish.

To Jennifer, to say that a house was a little one was to give it the highest praise. My father did not realise this when she made the remark: 'You live in a much smaller house than we do.' He replied with grim humour, 'Yes, but I don't have to take lodgers.'

When Tom was in Texas he sent Justyn a postcard saying, 'I am bringing you home a proper cowboy outfit with a huge hat and leather boots.' Justyn was so proud, he went round the different members of the staff saying, 'Please can you read this postcard for me, I don't read very well' to heighten the glory of his expectation.

Jennifer brought Justyn up and made life fun, as well as keeping him on the straight and narrow. He wouldn't bother to learn to read because, he told me, the stories Jennifer told him were more exciting than the ones in books! On one of his birthdays I overheard Jennifer's downright words to Justyn: 'You think it's fun having a birthday, don't you? Well, you wait. All the staff will ask you endless questions, and say something silly. But don't forget, you will answer every question politely—you mustn't let Daddy and Mummy down—then you can enjoy yourself after that.' Justyn meekly agreed. If it did make them behave rather like young adults, it was all part of life's discipline.

We decided it was not fair to bring up a small boy in such a restricted atmosphere, and so he went to boarding school when he was eight. We all felt the parting, but I think I found it most agonising. I asked if he would like to take a photo to school. He looked delighted, and I started to dig out a photo of Tom and myself, but found that what he wanted was a photo of his hamster!

Justyn had a mind of his own, and when the four of us had a meal together I often wondered what he was thinking as he looked at us with a measured glance. I found out later. He had decided that he was going to be different from the rest of us. Jennifer was a Christian, and father and mother, but this was not for him. Why should he become a Christian just because we were, so he looked at us with mental detachment.

We had theories about never frightening children with information about hell or the imminence of the Lord's Coming. In my youth the Second Coming was a threat rather than a glorious hope, and the nightmare of children brought up in evangelical homes was that the parents would go to heaven and they would find they had been left behind. A child would rather go to hell with his parents than to heaven without, and one can make a child embrace any religion if his security is threatened, so although we talked about heaven, and taught many Bible stories, judgment was soft-pedalled; I had not reckoned upon an enthusiastic guest who presented to Justyn a picture of the Two Ways. This was printed in 1870, and it fascinated both the children—the broad way presented vice and sin with lurid flames at the final destination. The narrow way had a rather godly boy with a Norfolk jacket, knickerbocker trousers, and a Bible under his arm. Jennifer kept urging Justyn to look at the flames, 'because that's where you're going because you're not a Christian,' she said.

Coming home from school, walking up the drive at Hildenborough with the Canadian redwoods, the tallest trees in Kent, on both sides, Justyn suddenly said, 'Jennifer, tell me how to become a Christian—I think it's time I did.' So Jennifer later told us, 'I took him behind a tree, and I told him to ask Jesus to come into his heart. He did, and it's permanent because he asked Him to come in forever. But,' she said, talking just as her father had done, more like a person of forty, 'I don't think he really understands what the Cross means. I'm going to think up some illustrations and tell him.'

I believe in child conversion. Whatever happened in the redwoods, at the next meal it was amazing to see the difference in Justyn. He told me afterwards, 'I looked round and thought we're all the same now—I'm a Christian, the same as the rest of you.'

In his early years it was my responsibility rather than Tom's to talk to the children concerning spiritual things, but when Justyn went to his public school there was a change. At his prep school he had started a Christian Union, calling it Pro Deo, the name he had learned from his father, and it was evident that he had an evangelistic urge. 'If I could just speak to the whole school once,' he told me. I asked him if he wouldn't be nervous. 'Nervous? Not a bit. I would tell them that being brought up in a Christian home isn't enough—you've got to make your own decision.'

Part of the Sunday afternoon ritual at home was a telephone call from his school. 'Justyn Rees is phoning you from Bath— will you accept the charge?' One Sunday Justyn sounded very agitated. 'I want to speak to the Boss,' he said, so I put Tom on. 'You'll have to help me,' Justyn said in a desperate tone. 'We had a talk at school on evolution, and I just don't believe anything now, you'll have to help me.' From this time Tom took over as far as Justyn was concerned. He talked to him quite calmly, and didn't attempt to argue, but as he had a little tape recorder, Tom said he would send him some tapes with positive reassuring teaching. I was interested when, in a recent television interview, Cardinal Heenan was asked, 'Did you have a time of doubt?' His answer was wise: 'Call it rather a time of questioning.' This was Justyn's experience, and Tom from then on helped in the answers.

There were, of course, the inevitable teenage clashes—'When is your son going to have his hair cut? Why must he wear those deplorable clothes?' Mothers are always the butt, of course, and I had to endure Justyn's black leather jackets as well as Tom's criticisms. I always understood that teenagers turned surly and awkward at some stage, but Justyn and Jennifer never did. I suppose they were more subtle; they knew just how to manage us. They agreed heartily if we complained about the untidy room. 'We are awful, Jennifer, aren't we?' Justyn would say, and she would say, 'We're frightful, but we will improve.'

Justyn endured school. He found the small restrictions futile, and it was no joy to him as he grew older to be allowed to leave another jacket button undone! He considered many prefects were unmannerly, shouting orders that he was perfectly happy to carry out.

I never thought when I spent five pounds on a Spanish guitar for his birthday that I was more than merely satisfying his latest craze. He was still at school, and when I imagined him at his studies, he was often in the music room teaching himself to play the guitar.

After he left school he went to Neuchâtel and Paris to learn French, and there was quite a shake-up when he returned from Paris with a diploma in French under one arm and his old guitar under the other. I didn't realise the extent to which he had studied the guitar until I arranged for him to have lessons, and discovered that he knew more than the teacher, and was soon teaching her! Nor did I realise that there were so many young people in the area until Justyn asked if he could have a Hallowe'en party. Up the road behind Hildenborough Hall we had an enclosed yard with several garages. I agreed that the party could be held there, so apples on strings, and turnip lanterns and plenty of doughnuts were provided. As the evening went on I wondered if all was well. Had they set the garage on fire—Were they rousing the neighbourhood? As I approached the premises there was a strange silence. I could see the flickering of the candles. Peeping through the crack I saw about fifty young people sitting quietly listening to Justyn. 'We have now come to the best part of the whole evening,' he told them. 'I want you to realise there is no need for any of you to go away not knowing that you're a Christian.'

They soon had a youth fellowship going, and sat in coffee bars conversing with young people, leading some of them to Christ. They discovered that most youngsters liked guitar music, so they formed a group—Justyn, with Jennifer and Tony Larcombe, Norman Miller, the bass guitarist, and a few others started to sing together. Tom invited the group to sing at the City Temple rallies that winter; they only knew two numbers, and sang them both, but week by week they learned new ones, most of them Justyn's compositions. For two years Justyn received tremendous experience in evangelism by travelling with the guitar group. They went into coffee bars, church halls, sang over the radio, and went to Ireland to appear on television. They prayed at least as much as they practised. It was in Scotland, camping by a loch, with only his dog for company, that Justyn composed one of his most effective numbers, 'Not now, but Tomorrow'.

Tom and I were anxious that Justyn would not follow in our footsteps. We had the call to Hildenborough, but we knew the hard work an total commitment that it involved, and were determined that Justyn should have a secular training. He wanted above all to learn to fly, but a temporary eyesight defect hindered this at seventeen, so he studied hotel management for three years, then discovered that his dream could be realised. He was accepted as a pilot, took his private pilot's licence in England, and decided to train in Florida as a commercial pilot

CHAPTER THIRTEEN

Tom and Billy

THE conferences and Royal Albert Hall rallies continued to complement each other. Thousands of people all over the world talked of Hildenborough and Tom's evangelistic meetings. The Royal Albert Hall became an integral part of London's plan of evangelism. In 1953 we had the help of Frank Boggs, whose superb voice and dedicated personality made a tremendous addition to the team, and we were all set for our fiftieth rally in 1954.

In March 1946 Tom had given a reception in the Bonnington Hotel to Torrey Johnson and his team from American Youth for Christ. They came to Hildenborough Hall for the night, and Tom was particularly attracted to one of the younger members of the party—Billy Graham. He thought he had great potential. He was right! Before Billy was nationally known he came over once or twice for Youth for Christ meetings, and had a mission in Lewisham. Maurice Rowlandson was Tom's assistant and chief cashier at Hildenborough, and he suggested that a few of us should go and hear Billy Graham.

Tom was away in Watford, and I was on the phone and mentioned casually that Maurice and I were taking a few of the staff to hear Billy 'to see what he's like'. I got what we called 'a blast'. 'You will not all go just to see what he's like,' Tom said. 'Don't go without earnest prayer for Billy and for souls, then you won't go in a critical spirit. Pray all the way through, back the preacher.' Duly subdued, we all tried to go in the right spirit. Maurice had worked with Tom in the Westminster Central Hall, and later joined us on the staff. He writes:

The Tom Rees I met as my boss was every bit as commanding a personality as the Tom Rees I had seen on the platform at the Central Hall. One quickly developed an overwhelming respect for his methodical approach to the business of running Hildenborough and evangelistic crusades and his utter integrity at every turn. Furthermore, he trusted his staff and gave them responsibility in a manner which others would have hesitated doing. He worked hard himself, and demanded the same devotion to duty from all of those who worked with him. He made few mistakes, and was sometimes a little intolerant of those who made foolish mistakes. However, one quickly learned that it was not intolerance, but training which he was giving, and which, looking back today, one is eternally grateful for. He was on easy terms with his staff, but nevertheless found it necessary at times to draw the line. Privately, he was Tom at all times, but in the business of Hildenborough he was always 'Mr. Rees' first, and as the years went by he came affectionately known as 'The Boss' to everyone, including his wife!

This was true. Although I was Tom's wife, I often forgot that. When Miss Hay and I ganged up against him in a perfectly friendly way over differences of opinion about the work we generally agreed amicably in the end. Miss Hay and I took a real pride in filling every bed at conferences, and sometimes to achieve this, we overbooked. Tom was adamant that there was to be no overcrowding, and sometimes when Miss Hay and I were surreptitiously having to fit in a few more guests, we were terrified 'The Boss' would find out. Miss Hay's comment in her Irish brogue was always, 'I tell you, the Boss will kill us.' I always quoted from 2 Kings, 'Then we can but die!'

It was in the full tide of the Albert Hall success that the suggestion was made that Billy Graham should come to London and have a crusade in Harringay. Tom readily agreed to cancel our 1954 series, and talking it over with Frank Boggs, said we would postpone our jubilee year. All through that conference season Tom took an evening out 'selling' the Harringay Crusade to young people. It seems strange now, but there was quite a considerable sales resistance. 'What, no Albert Hall—no choir?' Tom told them it would be a greater experience to sing under the leadership of Cliff Barrows. All our stewards and prayer partners were urged into action. Tom was delighted to have the opportunity of going on a tour to the West Country to start Bible groups in homes, already tremendously keen on this form of follow-up evangelism.

Tom and I loved Billy and Ruth, and we decided it was our special job to pray for them personally; to hedge them around against attacks from slander and opposition. Every car journey and spare moment we remembered them, but one or two people were evil enough to launch an attack on Tom attributing to him jealousy concerning Billy, and accusing him of opposing his visit, saying he was taking good care to be out of London while Billy was there. He was, however, anxious that evangelism and the name of the evangelist should not suffer. He knew that Billy and he were totally at one. He had strong opinions and expressed them, but his only jealousy was for the name of evangelism. He saw no reason why he should not express the fact that he did not like statistics of conversions. A London evening paper splashed 'Where are the 36,000 converts?' There were many converts, hundreds, thousands, but Tom thought it better to allow the Recording Angel to check the numbers.

Tom signed the contract for the 1955 Royal Albert Hall series, our jubilee year, before the news was released that Billy was to come back in 1955 for meetings at Wembley. We went ahead. From the moment Tom took his place on the platform, and Oliver Styles organised the vast congregation into singing 'Happy Jubilee to you', the wind was behind us, and the harvest was overwhelming.

In 1956 Tom realised Britain needed a time of consolidation. Large-scale evangelism for the time being had completed its cycle; he concentrated on Bible rallies, not only in London, but in such cities as Edinburgh, Carlisle, and Birmingham, revelling in a teaching ministry. He later had great rallies in London's City Temple, and the following year was a speaker at the Keswick Convention.

A letter from Billy Graham to his London headquarters concerning Tom's plans for 'Time for Truth' shows the trust between these two evangelists:

> I would like to give all-out support to our beloved friend, Tom Rees ... Tom is a man of God and I fully support him without any reservations. I am almost certain that we would have never come to the first Earls Court meeting had it not been for Tom's encouragement. When the decision was hanging in the balance he strongly urged me to accept the invitation.

In the States people would say to Tom, 'I understand you are the Billy Graham of Great Britain.' Tom always chuckled and replied, 'Not at all—Billy Graham's the Tom Rees of America!' There are several comments about Billy in Tom's diary—here's one: 'I have just had a time of prayer with Billy Graham. What a wonderful soul he is. Thank God for him, and for his ministry.'

After Tom died, Billy wrote inviting me to come over at his expense to stay with Ruth for a holiday. He had taken Tom's place in caring for a widow, the widow of a man who cared for so many other widows, but was not there to do so for me.

CHAPTER FOURTEEN

The 'Forty' Milestone

TOM's diaries at nineteen and in his early twenties were full of pent-up enthusiasm. In his thirties many of his ambitions were realised, but he could not settle down and allow himself any personal satisfaction from achievement. After reading Tom's book *His Touch has still its Ancient Power* the Duke of Windsor asked a friend, 'Is this man a humbug,' and when the reply was no, the Duke said, 'I would like to meet him.' Tom and I were invited to dine with friends, the Duke and Duchess of Windsor being the only other guests. We were told to call the Duke and Duchess 'Your Royal Highness' once, and subsequently to say 'Sir' or 'Madam', and I was advised to curtsey to both Duchess and Duke. After dinner Tom had a private chat with them.

I had first seen the Duke as Prince of Wales, the fair-headed young man who visited my native Newcastle. My father was closely connected with the organisation of the tour, and told us of the consternation caused when the Prince discovered there was a large hospital of badly wounded soldiers, and no visit had been planned. 'Change the programme,' demanded the Prince. 'I don't *have* to go to the races, do I?' He insisted on visiting a severely disfigured blind man and, after talking with him, actually kissed him. While Tom was talking to the Duchess, he asked me about the domestic staff at Hildenborough Hall. 'I understand that the staff at Buckingham Palace have a trade

112

union,' he told me, adding, 'I wouldn't have allowed that if I were still King.' The Duchess was charming, and told us with a broad smile, 'To the disappointment of a great number of people, the Duke and I are still very happy together.'

The following year after Tom's broadcast on Erling Olsen's New York programme, the switchboard operator in the Wall Street office was electrified to hear an English voice saying:

'Can I speak to Tom Rees? This is the Duke of Windsor speaking.'

'Oh yeah,' said the unbelieving telephonist. 'It's Queen Victoria here!'

The Duke invited Tom to the Tower Room of The Waldorf-Astoria. Unfortunately Tom was off to Chicago, but he had a long chat with His Royal Highness who wished him the utmost success.

The year Tom was forty was one of contrasts. On his fortieth birthday his comments are characteristic. 'Forty years old to-day, and I feel sixty. O that my youth could be renewed. Once I had youth and few opportunities; now I have many and great opportunities and no strength.' Forty is supposed to be the time of testing, when many settle into middle-aged mediocrity. Tom had a strong constitution, and only had to cancel three meetings through illness in the thirty-four years of our married life, but his diary shows increasingly the onset of fatigue. It should have cheered him up on his fortieth birthday to write, 'A conference of a hundred and twenty-six came in today, *forty* of them new Royal Albert Hall converts.'

He was right that he had many opportunities. During the previous year he had held the usual winter series at the Royal Albert Hall, with Bible Hours at St. Peter's, Vere Street. He spoke at the Young People's Convention at Belfast, the Keswick Convention, and a convention at Ballymena. Together with Canon Bryan Green he conducted a mission in Houston, Texas, organised by Bishop Quinn, the episcopal giant who topped his bishop's gaiters and apron with a cowboy hat! 'Hello boys,' he always greeted Bryan and Tom, and told the press the story of

H   113

his work as a bishop, and problems of the rivalry between the Episcopalians and the Baptists. A young Episcopal curate had wired him for advice: 'Have been asked to bury a Baptist. What shall I do?' Bishop Quinn wired back, 'Bury all you can!' That same year Tom conducted a mission in Guildford, and others in Canada. He broadcast extensively for the B.B.C. overseas programme, and this, of course, was all in addition to the Hildenborough conferences from Easter to October.

The Bible Hour meetings at St. Peter's, Vere Street were an excellent follow-up to the Royal Albert Hall, and gave people who had been contacted at the Albert Hall an opportunity of having Bible teaching and personal chats with Tom. Each Tuesday he was there until a late hour.

George, who worked at the Metropolitan Water Board, told Tom of a seven-year search for God. He had been sent to prison for being involved with some black market racket. 'The first five months,' he told Tom in his broad cockney, 'seemed like five years. One day me wife visited me, and said that a neighbour was praying for me. We both laughed, but that night,' he said, 'something happened to me in the middle of the night. I just knew that it was God. I didn't know anything about God, but suddenly I was so 'appy, I wouldn't leave me cell. I wouldn't go out for exercise. I said, "I'm not going out of 'ere because there's somethin' in 'ere, I don't know what it is, and if I go out, I'll lose it," so I stayed, and the last months in prison went like a flash. When they came and said, "George, it's time to go 'ome", I said "I'm in no 'urry. When I get out of 'ere I'll lose what I've got 'ere, cos I don't know what I've 'ad," and sure enough when I got 'ome it 'ad gone, but on Sunday I said to me wife, "Put yer 'at on, we're goin' to church. I've got to find out what it is that 'appened to me in prison." I went to church—'e didn't know what 'e was talking about, so at night I said to me wife, "Put yer 'at on, we're going out to church." She said, "What again?" I said, "we're going to church every Sunday until I find what I've 'ad." I went on every Sunday, morning and evening for seven years, and I never found what

114

I was lookin' for. I went to 'ear bishops, I went to 'ear anyone that spoke about anythin' religious, but I didn't find the man that could tell me.

'Then,' he said, 'last week me mate said to me, 'e said, "Will you come with me to the Albert Hall?" I said "I don't care for that—I'm not much of a one for listenin' to people fiddlin'." "It's not fiddlin'—'e's talking about Get Right With God." I said "Is it religious?" He said "yes". I said, "Right, it might be 'im," because one of these days I knew I'd find 'im, "and then the man can tell me what it is I've 'ad, that I 'ad in prison." The Sunday before that, me wife 'ad said to me "Give it up". She said "you've tried for seven years." But I said, "If you knew what it was that I 'ad in prison, you'd know that if I went on every Sunday for the rest of me life, I'd 'ave to go on searching!" I went to the Albert 'all. I sat there in the front. You came on the platform, and you said one word before you announced your 'ymn. I shoved me poor wife in her ribs—she 'adn't said anything. "Shut up," I said, "it's 'im. Listen," and I knew it was 'im. I listened to what you 'ad to say and it was all that I 'ad in prison. I said to meself, don't rush, I said, you go to that Tuesday evening thing and find out all about it, so 'ere I am, and I want you to tell me what it is that I 'ad, and what it is that you've got because I want to 'ave it.'

Tom led George to the Lord, and afterwards he said, 'Yes, I've got it now,' and he tapped his lower chest—'I've got it just there, just where you've got it. I don't 'ave the same feelings, but they don't matter. I've got what I searched for.'

Tom maintained that when someone became a Christian, it was always the result of prayer. 'Who was praying for you?' he asked a young man after an Albert Hall rally, when the actor, John Byron, told Tom of his conversion. 'No one,' said John, 'I do not know of a single person who prayed for me.' He was wrong.

For the beginning of the story we go a long way back. My youngest sister was doing 'O' levels in English, and I took her to Stratford specially to see *Hamlet*. Tom, the complete puritan, looked at me doubtfully, but he believed in 'live and let live'. My sister completely fell for Hamlet as portrayed by John Byron. 'What a Christian he would make,' she said, and promptly started to pray for him. How wrong I was to be so cynical, while saying 'Yes, do that.' So prayer was put into the spiritual bank of John Byron, and a few years later an over-whelming desire for Christ took hold of his inner being. He did not know of a single Christian person, but one Sunday morning he got up determined to go to church and find out. He espied a lady with a Bible and a Prayer Book, and 'shadowed' her. This lady realised she was being followed, and John had to confess that he felt she would lead him to church. She unbent. 'I am going to All Souls, Langham Place,' she said. 'You may come with me.' In conversation she admitted that she was a nanny at the home of the Polish Ambassador. 'I have had all the Ambassador's children', she told the astonished John, who realised she meant something quite different from the world in which he lived. He was a very successful television actor taking part in what was the Sunday Night Play, as well as touring with the Shakespeare Company. After an Albert Hall rally Tom said to me:

'I want you to meet John Byron, he has just recently become a Christian.'

Like Livingstone meeting Stanley, I said, 'Hamlet, I presume!'

Tom was very tolerant about what other people permitted. He didn't judge a person's Christianity by outward actions, 'tithing mint and rue like the Pharisees'. However, although Tom was indifferent about the prohibitions and shibboleths of others, he had a rigid code for himself. He'd had his fill of films and shows, and found them futile. He kept himself from anything that would detract from his aim and object—to know Christ and serve Him. The Nazarites in the Old Testament took a vow to refrain not only from wine, but from the skin and stone of the grape. This was quite optional, and Tom, in his comparatively short life, wholly followed the Lord. He hated television with a detestation that I considered quite unreasonable, because, let me admit, I enjoyed the relaxation of it. Tom's mother and I often enjoyed a programme together, but she said to me once, 'Isn't it strange, we can be watching something quite innocent, but it only wants Tom to come in, for someone either to take all their clothes off, or to get into bed with the wrong people!' It was quite true—Tom would come in with 'Good life, is this what you've been watching? What a way to spend your time.' I often told him it was his duty to watch something at least once a week to keep in touch with life, so he agreed to come and watch the commercials because he said they were quite the best part!

The year he was forty there were encouragements. Before the Royal Albert Hall series he wrote, 'I am feeling in the depths of depression re: the Albert Hall series.' On the day of the first rally he wrote, 'Hardly slept at all. Rose at 5.00 a.m.' His reports of the rally were unusually cheerful: '5,000 stayed to the after-meeting, and there were at least a hundred really encouraging conversions.' The results continued to be encouraging. 'Had a record number of cards,' but adds cautiously, 'not that this means much.' It is only to his diary that Tom mentions numbers. The very expression 'registered decisions' made his hackles rise.

During this year Tom spoke at a rally on the south coast, and was available afterwards to talk with people who had found Christ. After chatting with a good-looking eighteen-year-old who had become a Christian during the meeting, Tom thought he was being the victim of a practical joke when two other identical young men came forward. They were triplets, and independently from different parts of the church had accepted Christ.

Friday, July 13th was not an unlucky day. Tom thanked the Lord in his diary with a hearty Amen! and Hallelujah! because the accounts for the Royal Albert Hall showed that the costs had been £6,000, and the receipts showed a balance of £100. 'God is good,' he comments.

At the end of July we went to the Solway coast with the family for a short holiday. Tom's brother, Dick, came and joined us for a day or two, and we talked until late, discussing revival. I had just been reading the life of C. G. Finney, who said, 'Any group could have a revival if they were willing to pay the price, in utter holiness, prayer, and adjustment of lives.' We argued to and fro, academically and mentally, but that night the whole idea hit me. I was in my fortieth year, and Tom was forty. Humanly speaking we could expect to have about thirty years of service, but what we needed was a middle year booster, a further call, a revival. We had already been blessed, but even though we were indwelt by the Holy Spirit, it was possible to let Him have more of us.

I thought of the B.B.C. broadcast from the Hildenborough Hall lounge. The room normally held 150 at the outside, but we had packed in two hundred by removing the cumbersome sofas and armchairs. Tom had often spoken about this, and so had I. 'All right,' I said, 'we'll give it a chance.' I had more 'sofas' to turn out than Tom. Life was transformed for me, and Tom seemed to get new strength for the challenges ahead.

I had accepted the fact that we could not hope to have a separate home, but there was still a hungry desire for a little bit more of Tom. Some time before, as an act of faith, I had asked the Lord to deepen my love for Tom, but to stop me being so 'in love' with him. I found it agony never to be together, so rarely to eat together, only at snatched holidays, which made the ache worse afterwards. This, in a measure, God did for me, but during that year when we had been married fifteen years I came to another crisis. I went to Switzerland with my mother and Jennifer and had time to think and pray about our future life. At first I told myself it was lovely having a holiday with only females, I could look at the shops without being hustled; but after a few days my whole soul was crying out for Tom. I decided I could go on no longer with our way of life. I could not exist without having more of Tom, and some home life, so I wrote him a long letter and committed the matter to

God in prayer. I had much to be thankful for; Tom wanted above everything to be with me, and holidays together were his delight, and when parted he wrote every day. We had not grown apart, but ...

Tom often said to me, 'Don't die first, or I'll be so covered with remorse,' but for a perfectionist to be married to me must have been hard. He liked garage doors shut, and I left them open. He tried very hard to reform me. My mother told him he was trying to turn a wood into a park in organising my character, and Tom said he didn't mind the wood, but he wanted to prevent it from becoming a jungle!

I waited for Tom's reply to my letter, but matters that are big to the female mind are not so big to a man planning evangelistic programmes and conferences. He read my letter, put the contents in his subconscious mind, and left them there. It always made his heart sink when he got a very long letter from me written in very good writing!

Tom often told the story of a small boy who lost his marble and could not get on with his homework. He asked Auntie if he could stop his lessons and pray that he could find it. Later Auntie asked, 'Did God answer your prayer and help you to find your marble?' Johnnie said, 'Yes, God answered my prayer. I didn't find the marble, but God made me not want it any more.'

God answered my prayer by sending a revival in my soul. The Lord became a greater reality, my satisfaction in the work multiplied, and a greater love for souls filled the gap. On our fifteenth anniversary, when Tom and I went into Knole Park and spent some considerable time in prayer, and later had a meal at Penshurst, I realised that God had answered my prayer abundantly. God is good. There is a verse that I am very aware of. It says, 'God granted them their request, but sent leanness into their souls.' He had given us both a fresh impetus for the middle years, and what a spiritual harvest we saw in the conference and evangelistic work!

The reason Tom did not discuss our life together was, I am

sure, because he was uncertain about the future. Should we continue organising conferences? Could we cope physically? Perhaps my letter to him made him realise I had been at the end of my tether. We could have sold the conference centre as a going concern. This particular year was the only time when we ever finished on the right side financially—only by a very small amount, I think it was £200, but at least we were holding our own. Tom felt that we should form a non-profit-making Trust, so there could be no risk of anyone saying we did it for personal gain. It was extraordinary how quite intelligent people think. They added up the gross receipts of one peak week, and multiplied it by fifty-two, and decided we were running a gold mine. The empty winter weeks were quite forgotten. When Tom was conducting a mission in a Scottish city, having paid his own hotel bill and expenses, he suggested having an informal meeting to show the Hildenborough film, telling young people about the conferences, particularly the new converts. A member of the committee was loud in condemnation, and refused to permit Tom to use the mission to advertise his money making concern! Tom was impervious to criticism from the outside world, but he was very sensitive to criticism from his fellow workers, and he suddenly wondered if others felt that Hildenborough Hall was a financial asset. When I thought of the sacrifice, of the hard work, and the results, I was angry, but Tom quietly put plans in motion to form The Hildenborough Evangelistic Trust.

I had misjudged him about his silence concerning my letter. It had gone into his subconscious and borne fruit. He planned that we should have a flat of our own, putting a door on one of the landings, thus making a private apartment. It was wonderful —a small insurance scheme matured when I was forty, so we could afford to furnish and equip. It gave the children a greater sense of security, and on several occasions Tom and I actually had an evening together! He enjoyed the meals I cooked, and was so appreciative. 'Your shepherd's pie is better than anyone else's roast turkey,' he told me.

CHAPTER FIFTEEN

Frinton-on-Sea

So we formed Hildenborough into a non-profit-making charitable Trust. Although we had only once made an infinitesimal profit in ten years, we thought it was better to make the lack of profit official! The Bishop of Barking, later the Archbishop of Sydney, became our President, with Lt.-Gen. Sir William Dobbie, the Rev. Geoffrey King, and the Rev. Dr. W. E. Sangster as our Vice-Presidents. We chose a few friends to work with us on the Business Executive. We wanted men who not only had business ability, but who knew all about the work, and what we were aiming at, so Mr. Cyril Wiggins, a builder, who was heart and soul behind the evangelistic and conference work was a must.

I was talking with him only the other day. He said: 'People just take evangelistic activity for granted now, but Tom really started everything after the war. Hildenborough was the first of all the conference centres; the evangelistic efforts in London and the whole of the south-east came alive from that date.'

Robert Johnson also joined us. He not only had an important position in the Metal Box Company, but also in the Ministry of Food. His spiritual counsel and advice were invaluable. At one meeting Tom said, 'What do you all feel about it?' and Robert replied, 'Well, you're the meteor—we're just the tail. Go right ahead, and we'll follow you.'

121

It was rather wonderful that he was in New York in the few days following Tom's homecall, and so was able to attend the service that Stephen Olford conducted in the Salisbury Hotel.

David Rennie, an engineer, together with David Hanton, a solicitor, completed our Executive. It was only a short time after its formation that together we had to make a big decision.

Immediately after the war the seaside was not a popular place for a holiday. We connected it with threatened invasions, barbed wire fences and concrete blocks, but after nearly ten years at a country mansion, in spite of glorious trees and the lake, everyone hankered again for the sea.

No one in their senses would have moved from Kent to the seaside in one day: would have ended one conference on a Friday night, and after singing heartily, 'we thank Thee for all that is past ...' motored a hundred miles to Frinton-on-Sea, to be prepared at tea time the next day to open a new conference. We sang the rest of the hymn ... 'and trust Him for all that's to come.' The secret was that, although we had fifteen Pickford pantechnicons full of furniture to be taken from Hildenborough Hall in Kent to Hildenborough Hall in Essex, it was not transported overnight, for the new conference centre was rented furnished.

We found the property by accident. Having searched all the south coast resorts as far as Bournemouth in the west, on returning from a trip to East Anglian seaside towns we found Frinton, a peaceful paradise where there were no piers, cinemas, or picnicking on the greensward.

There were many anxieties but we found a good purchaser, a doctor who agreed to take over Hildenborough Hall as a convalescent home. Then the County Council, in a very high-handed manner, decided to buy it, threatening compulsory purchase if we refused.

There were terrible moments. When we had committed ourselves to Frinton and made all the plans, the County Council representatives responsible for the purchase of the original

Hildenborough said quite casually that they hadn't looked at the roof. If there was anything wrong with that, the sale was off.

In the meanwhile we had been compelled to say no to the doctor who had offered to purchase.

'But you contracted to purchase,' Tom said,

'Oh no, we never have a contract in a compulsory purchase.'

'But you haven't got a compulsory purchase, you only threatened to do so.'

'It's the same thing,' he said.

We were stunned, very tired, and I suppose we should have gone blithely on saying, 'It is all in the plan, and the Lord will provide,' but the thought of having two enormous properties on our hands did cause us to experience a considerable sinking feeling, and we were quite unable to quote glibly to each other 'If we worry, we don't trust, and if we trust, we don't worry,' or any of those other aggravating things that people quote when it is not their worry.

Happily the roof was pronounced sound, and Tom and I wondered again when we would learn to trust. After we moved we still had our worries. In November the County Council were in possession of the Kent house, but when we said a cheque would be welcome, they said they hadn't received final permission from the Ministry of Health, and of course, if that was not forthcoming, again the sale would be off.

Tom and I were away having a short break, but it was difficult to relax knowing that bills were piling up. Tom recited a little couplet which always encouraged him:

He Who has taught us to trust in His Name
Would not so far have brought us to put us to shame.

Just before Christmas the Council paid part of their debt, and again we wondered why we had worried.

Life at Frinton was different, but delightful. There were four evangelical churches in the town. What a contrast it was being right on the sea front, instead of in the heart of the country. Tom often came home covered with embarrassment, having given cheery greetings to those he thought were members of a houseparty, but getting icy glances from strangers who thought he was a little bit fresh.

We had a delightful Scandinavian party one year, and at the welcome session Tom made everyone relax including some from the States and the Continent, while we compared the greetings each different nation used. The Americans said 'Hi', our French student said 'Salut', we in England say 'Hello', and our friends from Sweden told us that they say 'Hey'. A late arrival was a tall, fair-haired lady who looked like a headmistress. On her way to breakfast the next day Tom, assuming that she was Swedish, acting the genial host, said in a hearty manner 'Hey'. She gave him a stony glance and replied, 'Good-morning'. He said 'Hey' again, slightly hesitatingly, and still persisting asked, 'What would you say was the literal translation of 'Hey', to which she replied, without batting an eyelid, 'I would say it was dried grass.'

We spent five very happy years at Frinton, successful times numerically, satisfactory times financially, and spiritually most rewarding.

With more accommodation, and the sea only a few yards away, large parties from churches were brought by their ministers. We had family parties each June. With the beach adjacent it was a children's paradise.

It was a difficult decision to make after five years, whether to renew the lease of the Esplanade Hotel, which we called Hildenborough Hall, or whether to concentrate on evangelism. Five years had elapsed since Billy Graham's Harringay and Wembley crusades, and evangelism in Britain was again on the upsurge. The conference work had been so demanding yet full of opportunity.

After the consolidating years with Bible rallies and conventions, Tom felt the urge to go out and 'offer Christ freely to the people' as Wesley put it. We decided not to renew the lease of the large premises, but to retain the adjoining house, Hildenborough Lodge, as an evangelistic centre from which to organise his work.

CHAPTER SIXTEEN

To Every Corner
of Britain

JAMES had been a clever boy at school, successful in an appointment abroad, and finding himself in London, wandered into St. Paul's Cathedral. It was packed to capacity. A service was in progress, and people were standing in every available place.

'What's on?' he asked.

'It's a service for Tom Rees, the famous preacher,' he was told. 'He's going round the country preaching, and they're having a Dedication Service.'

'Tom Rees,' said James thoughtfully. 'I was at school with a Tom Rees, but it couldn't be him. He couldn't be a famous *anything*.'

'There he is,' said the verger, as Tom was led to the lectern to read the New Testament lesson. James looked with open mouth. It *was* Tom Rees—the chap at the bottom of the lower fourth—reading, 'Kept by the power of God through faith unto salvation.'

'I've seen everything,' James told the verger. 'There's hope for *anyone* if Tom Rees can become a famous preacher.'

The Bishop of Barking conducted the service, assisted by Prebendary Colin Kerr. The Rev. John Stott, Rector of All Souls, Langham Place, and one of the Queen's chaplains, gave a never-to-be-forgotten message.

As Tom read, 'Ye rejoice with joy unspeakable and full of

126

glory,' the bell of Great Tom clanged out 7 o'clock, and Tom remembered the message on the skirt of the bell, 'Woe is me if I preach not the gospel.'

I will not dwell on Tom's missions, conventions, and crusades in Winnipeg, Victoria, and Vancouver; in Seattle, Washington; New York and Texas with Canon Bryan Green; throughout Great Britain, including conventions such as Keswick and Portstewart; but the Mission to Britain I will write about, as it shows so many aspects of Tom.

If the three years at Banwell were the happiest of our lives, the eight months when Tom took the Gospel message to within fifty miles of every person in Great Britain, visiting ninety-eight counties and 158 centres, were to him the most satisfying. We saw God maintain us spiritually, support us financially, inspiring us with memories, and strengthening our faith for every future effort.

Tom wrote to *The Life of Faith*: 'In almost every rally God has guided me to preach strongly and plainly about man's need and the wrath of God against sin. His Word has been "as a fire shut up in my bones." I have not been conscious of the fact that I was preaching a sermon, but rather that I was delivering a message.'

As usual I have started the story in the middle, so must go back to when something was first brewing in Tom's mind. He had felt led, after the mammoth Harringay and Wembley crusades following his ten years of Royal Albert Hall rallies, to concentrate on Bible teaching, but God had not given him the gift of an evangelist for nothing.

The conferences at Hildenborough carried on relentlessly and fruitfully. I use the word 'relentlessly' deliberately. They started at Easter, and continued through to October.

Tom not only did a Bible Rally in Westminster Chapel on Saturday nights, but also a marathon tour, including visits to Bedford, Carlisle, Falkirk and Edinburgh, 1,100 miles a week for nine weeks, giving talks on the Book of the Acts, later published in *The Church Marches In*. As if this was not enough, he included missions in Inverness and Bradford, and where I take up the story he was planning the following winter to visit Edinburgh, Glasgow, Dundee, Bristol and Birmingham before returning to London.

Christian workers like ourselves who frequently work a sixteen-hour day (and are privileged to do so) do not have a heavenly trade union, and in order to escape the mental pressure of the conference centre, Tom and I, with Miss Hay and Elizabeth, had gone out in the car with our notebooks and pencils, leaving no message of our whereabouts in order to talk and plan. By 8 p.m. we were feeling as if we had already visited these far flung places, and were somewhat exhausted.

If some difficult information had to be given to anyone, I often said, 'Let me explain.' Tom was a very poor salesman unless he was presenting the Gospel. Mother always taught me that if you have to break anything difficult to your husband, never do it at breakfast. No one had ever given Tom such helpful information, and when we were quite exhausted and very hungry, he said blandly, 'Would you like me to tell you what we will be doing the next winter?' The question was quite rhetorical, for he went on, 'I plan to visit every county in England, Ireland, Scotland and Wales, having one or two rallies in each county, visiting not only places where we shall be welcomed, but where there will be no local committee, and where we will go in a really pioneering spirit. It will probably take about six months.'

To our credit we did not react as we might have done. Our comments were all characteristic. Elizabeth, who was in charge of the accounts at Hildenborough, said 'It will need some financing.' I said, 'You will need a really first class organiser,' and Miss Hay, lapsing into Irish brogue, as she does in times of stress, said fervently, 'It's praying for you'll be needing.'

Even to write about this wonderful mission makes my heart glow. Imagine planning to cover in quite a short space of time 1,200 miles from London (St. Paul's) back to London (the Royal Albert Hall), visiting every corner of the British Isles.

Every bit of our brain and ingenuity was needed to prepare the conference centre called Hildenborough Hall. (*Below*) An aerial view.

Setting off to visit every county in Britain: Tony Groom, Tom Rees, Ian Cory, Jean Rees, Joyce Silcox, and Elizabeth Smith.

On the road, preaching within fifty miles of every person in Britain.

Ian and Rachel Cory with a Mission to Britain poster.

Going along the south coast, taking in the Isle of Wight and the Channel Islands; through Devon and Cornwall, back again to the West Midlands, the Border County of Wales; through every county of Wales itself, over to Northern Ireland in the beginning of 1959, down to Dublin; to the Isle of Man, up through western Scotland, visiting the Kyles of Bute, then to the Highlands to Fort William, so on through Inverness to the most northerly point for a rally at Wick, flying to Stornoway in the Outer Hebrides, and then down by the east coast to Edinburgh, and back visiting the Midlands, the eastern counties of England through Yorkshire, East Anglia, and finally to the mass rally in the Royal Albert Hall on May 16th.

The route was planned and the local secretaries chosen. After futile searching for an organiser it was Elizabeth Smith who told Tom that given one more helper, she could cope at headquarters; and how wonderfully she did. Elizabeth had a brain like a man, but Tom said she was able to do the work of two men. Never on any experience of planning evangelistic enterprises were so many telephone calls and so many letters written in so short a time. The posters alone weighed four and a half tons, and these were only a small part of the printing and publicity.

Tom and I had our personal anxieties. He was very keen that I should travel with him on this tour. I did not generally do so on his marathon trips around the country, only to the main centre, but during the previous winter Jennifer had been very ill. She had outgrown her strength, and each winter some virus attacked her, and any slight infection, even a cold, laid her low for some months. The previous winter when Tom was in Canada we nearly lost her, and if I went on this tour I wanted to bring her. Just before we left I see in my diary, kept for nearly twenty years, 'Am sick with anxiety. Have caught a slight cold, and if I give this to Jennifer we have had it.' I believe in healing that glorifies the great Physician who answers prayer.

At a Homemakers' Conference in September I had confided

my anxiety to some of the guests, and Miss Pettifer, sister of Robert Pettifer the evangelist who preceded Tom to Glory, wrote and told me, 'I have decided to make Jennifer's health my burden for the Mission to Britain. I am praying that both Jennifer and you and your husband will be kept in health and strength throughout the tour.' For the first winter for many years Jennifer did not have a cold, and after preaching six days a week, often several times a day, Tom never even had a sore throat. In fact, Ian Cory wrote concerning Tom's health: 'His wife maintains that he is in better health and spirits than at any time in their twenty years of married life!'

On the field, travelling from place to place, Ian Cory was field director and organiser, and general progress chaser. Driving his mini-bus he took Gordon Brattle, the pianist (in private life, a dentist); Joyce Silcox, Tom's secretary; and travelling like an outrider on a Lambretta, was Tony Groom who had organised the geographical possibilities of the tour. Other people joined us from time to time including Nigel Cooke whom we first met as a teenager and who later became a staff member, and today as a businessman is the Vice-Chairman of The Hildenborough Evangelistic Trust, together with Claire London, my secretary, and Frank Boggs, the soloist.

Ian organised everyone. He told them they must bring only one case, which must not weigh more than forty-five pounds. Tony Groom, who never uses one syllable if three will do, explained to Ian that on his perambulations and peregrinations he would be quite unable to convey personal impediment from one domicile to the next, so Ian graciously afforded him a space in the mini-bus. Tony Groom with his long words was a constant amusement to us all. He described the Mission to Britain, according to Ian Cory, as a 'protracted project of gargantuan proportions, which embraces in its prehensile purview the indigenous inhabitants of the conurbations and agricultural communities contained in our insural domicile.' In brief, Ian explained, 'Round Britain Whizz!'

Tom had to have a first class pianist. His Welsh soul was

not able to tolerate anything but the best, and a pianist whose harmonies were not correct grated on Tom. It was an answer to all our prayers when Gordon was able to have leave of absence from his dental practice to join us.

At this pre-tour committee meeting conducted by Ian we all received a preview of what was to come. I explained that we were planning to have a main meal at our host and hostess's house about six o'clock, as it would be rather late to have a main meal after the rally. Gordon explained that he would be happy to have a main meal both before and after the rally! He is an amazing person who can eat anything at any hour of the day or night and generally does. Ian stood no nonsense at this point and reminded them all that everyone had to get to bed as soon as possible, and that the rule of the party was that everyone had to be in bed by eleven o'clock. (It reminded me of when I first met Tom.)

After the service in St. Paul's we set off. We were kept from exhaustion because Tom was not dealing with staff problems, conference needs, financial anxieties, and future planning. We travelled on to the next place, arriving about 3 p.m., and if I had a women's meeting, or Tom a ministers' tea, we went to that while Ian and party disgorged the hymn books and Joyce and Claire arranged the flowers. Gordon tried out the piano, and all went to high tea at the place of our new hospitality. We arrived at the rally, and after community singing the members of the party introduced themselves, Joyce sang, and Tom gave his message. At the end Tom conducted what he called an 'Act of Witness'.

'Drawing in the net' is something that concerns the minds, hearts, and consciences of evangelists perpetually. Tom had very strong convictions that there must be no trickery, undue pressure, or unwise use of emotion. If anyone 'came out' it must mean something; enquirers had an opportunity of coming forward later with the counsellors. He asked anyone who had accepted Christ that night, or in the previous year, or sometimes two years, according to the place, to come forward and confess their faith. This was not popular with many who said, 'I like to count the number who were converted that night.' ('How many decisions tonight?' someone asked Tom. 'Ask the recording angel when we get to heaven, and he'll look it up for you,' Tom answered.) This Act of Witness was a great encouragement to ministers and Bible class leaders who realised that through their faithful ministry and teaching, quietly at a church service, or in a confirmation class, young people have accepted Christ without the courage to say so. This Act of Witness enabled them to be followed up. Tom considered this much better than the old-fashioned 'eyes closed—heads bowed —no one looking, everyone peeping' method!

In the after-meeting Tom divided those who were converted that night and those of recent months, and this gave Ian Cory the opportunity of talking with recent converts, asking about Bible study, witness and progress, while Tom and the rest of us talked to those who had just come to Christ. It was astonishing in this particular tour to find how many had clearly been converted through the preaching, and needed little counselling, understanding things clearly.

A boy in Bristol had come simply because he had seen the poster 'Get Right with God'. 'If I could find a man who could show me how to get right with God I would be happy,' he said. He came to the rally, listened to the message, and at the end of the meeting responded when Tom asked those who had accepted Christ to come forward. Nigel Cooke told us that when he asked him if he was quite clear about salvation, the young man said earnestly, 'I am right with God by His grace, because Christ died for me, and I have put my faith in Him.' It is amazing how someone can take in so much the first time they hear the gospel message.

Most mornings we all went to the mission office, set up in a church vestry, and at 10 a.m. began our prayer meeting. At this there was a sense of urgency, and although at lunch we became more hilarious, at the prayer meeting Tom had us all in check. At first we would share the joys and miracles of the previous night. Ian Cory could tell us in Dover of the young reporter whose conversion he had prayed for throughout the rally, and who became a Christian. I might tell of a Roman Catholic girl who, with glowing face, said, 'Do I only have to ask?' Ian also told us about the Scotsman who, after the meeting, was apparently searching for something. 'Are you trying to find the way out?' asked Ian politely. 'No,' said the Scotsman, 'I am trying to find the Lord.' He was eighty-three, and a few years previously during a serious illness, thinking that he was dying, had started to seek the Lord. When he saw the poster 'Get Right with God' he took this as his opportunity and went away with a knowledge of salvation.

In Swindon a woman was introduced to me by Joyce, who in a stage whisper, said, 'This woman has a horrible brutal husband who ill-treats her, and I am sure *you* will be able to help her!'

Tom was a firm leader. 'Your playing was superb last night, Gordon,' he would say. 'You excelled yourself. Pity you fell over the mike lead when you went to introduce yourself!' 'Tony and Jean, you were both too long as usual on your introductions. We can't spare the time. If, instead of saying 'perambulations and peregrinations' you could say 'tour' it would save time; still, you were both bang on, and so were you Joyce. Sing that one again tonight, or what had you in mind? Keep her going a bit faster, Gordon.' Any little failure in the organisation never escaped his eye, but he was full of appreciation.

Early in the tour we found that people sympathised with us, and said we looked exhausted, and we felt this was a bad witness, so Claire, Joyce, and I bought a pot of rouge and some glucose tablets, and arrived looking in beaming health, then a friend gave us all a huge box of vitamin pills, and Joyce doled these out at lunch time. We decided that the words 'tired' and 'exhausted' were not to be in our vocabulary. It was extraordinary that if we did not tell each other we were tired, that we were not tired. Ian told us that they got just as tired on a hockey tour (he had his Blue for this).

We usually had lunch together, provided by kind ladies in the church hall. Tom had written to all the centres saying that a simple lunch would be welcome, something like ham and salad, so ham and salad it was almost every day for eight months. Tony Groom said that my book about the mission should be called 'Salad Days'.

We never had a quarrel or any unpleasantness, but endless fun. When Joyce had her jewellery stolen at Fort William, and detectives suspected the rest of the party, particularly Tom and Ian who were flying to Stornoway the next day (Who would go to the Hebrides in February?) the fun kept us going for days. When they called in the Navy to send down frogmen because the thief had thrown them in the Loch, it was like a serial story, especially as Joyce had mentally spent the insurance money. When the jewellery was recovered and the value was discovered to be sentimental rather than intrinsic, the disgust of the police and the navy knew no bounds!

Travelling swiftly as we did gave us a chance to compare spiritual reactions in different places. So often the response depended on the amount of prayer, preparation, and imaginative planning. Some rallies were what Tom called 'the merry-go-round' type—just one of a series of spiritual picnics. After one surprise harvest we found that for some weeks a number of people had covenanted to rise at 5.30 a.m. for prayer.

My father was at one of our rallies. He was very correct in his theological terms, and had frequently told us that Revelation 3:20, 'Behold, I stand at the door and knock', should not be used for people coming to Christ—it was dispensationally wrong, the verse was spoken to the Church. At this rally our experience was like the miraculous draught of fishes; we had to beckon to our partners to help us, and Tom asked Father to talk to a schoolboy who wanted to accept Christ. Father came back beaming, the boy had got salvation good and proper. I asked Father if he used any particular verse to lead the boy to Christ. He looked very shamefaced and admitted that he had used Revelation 3 : 20, 'but I still think it's not for this dispensation, it's for the Church,' he said. 'I know,' I told him, 'but it worked, didn't it?'

Friday was Press day. After lunch those of us who wrote articles for the various Christian papers read our accounts to the team for comments and criticism. Tom was very down on any exaggeration. Tony Groom would read, 'The hall was full ...' 'Say it was well filled, Tony. There were a few empty seats at the back.' Tony docilely agreed, and when Ian said the hall was packed out, Tom suggested he said 'It was full.' When Ian maintained there had been people in the aisle and a few outside, he was allowed to proceed. In my turn I read, 'To a congregation of nearly a thousand ...' 'How d'you know there was nearly a thousand?' Tom asked. Rather acidly, 'Because I counted head by head up to 980 during your third point,' I said. 'I might have known,' Tom replied. 'I knew I'd lost them at that point.'

At Swansea a few girls were chattering at the back, and Tom asked them very kindly to listen. The local reporter seized on that eagerly, and there were large headlines concerning the evangelist's 'obvious irritability' in rebuking the members of the congregation who whispered. The following day there was a storm of letters to the editor from people who had been present. 'I was in the front pew,' wrote someone, 'and failed to see any irritability on the part of the evangelist when he rebuked a few members of the congregation. I thought he did it graciously and with the authority of Scripture. I think the reporter failed to realise that the evangelist is God's instrument by standing between life and death, and souls were deciding their future destiny. God would have reverence, and it's time congregations were rebuked for their behaviour in the presence of the Lord.'

When Tom saw a congregation before him, choosing life or death, it was inevitable that he demanded the attention of his hearers. I was rather amused by a letter we received from a minister after one of the rallies thanking us for sending him the names of fourteen people who had professed conversion the previous night. He said there was one criticism he would like to make. He thought it would be better if Mr. Rees did not say to the congregation 'Listen to me' or 'Hear me' to demand their attention. 'It would have been better to preach and leave it at that.' I could not help wondering whether, if Tom had been less forthright, the minister would have had fourteen names to follow up.

People like George Whitefield did not tolerate inattentive congregations. Once a man in front of the pulpit fell asleep during Whitefield's preaching. 'All at once he stopped short, his countenance changed, and he broke forth: "If I had come to speak to you in my own name, you might well rest your elbows on your knees and your heads on your hands and sleep, but I have come to you in the Name of the Lord of Hosts." Here he brought his hand and foot down with such force that he made the building ring. "I must, and will be heard," he said. The old man woke up at once.'

We had a press conference with many of the leading papers, including *The Times*, *The Manchester Guardian*, *The Scotsman*, and the *Daily Mirror* before we set out on our tour. They were looking for a headline rather than for news. The *Daily Mirror* reporter was charming, and interviewed me privately. All he wanted to know was how much more Billy Graham earned than Tom Rees. In public the main burden of the questions seemed to be to get Tom to say something against Billy Graham. 'Was it right for him to have so much money? How did their methods differ?' When Tom expressed himself not only as an admirer of Billy Graham, but as a personal friend, interest died.

I remember having a long exhausting interview with a representative from *John Bull*, who tried to make me tell of ways in which Tom was awkward or difficult. In desperation I gave him a copy of my first book *Putting Ten Thousand to Flight*. I said, 'In here you will get all the information you'll need.' He took it, and returned it to me later with profuse thanks, saying how interesting he had found it. I discovered that it was a copy of the book where the pages had not been cut!

There were many high spots like the vast rally in Liverpool where we had to change from the Philharmonic Hall to a boxing arena to accommodate the crowds.

There was the tiny town of Llandyssul in Wales, where Tom's grandfather was born, and where the 'chef de gare promenaded himself'; hundreds of people climbed up the steep slope to the Sein Congregational church, the special police constable controlling the traffic. In the town of 990 inhabitants, a thousand people came to the rally.

All the way through this wonderful tour Tom's zeal and zest never flagged. On by far the majority of occasions his sermon was Romans 3. This message so gripped Tom's heart that he only preached on any other subject for very shame, and out of consideration for his fellow workers. 'There is no difference—all have sinned; ... there is none that doeth good, no not one.'

I marvelled that when Tom preached this sermon it should still be so fresh. I was never tired of hearing it. In a large Yorkshire city I called for him to come and have some high tea. 'I can't come,' he said, 'I must prepare, I don't want a meal.' I realised that this would mean his having to exist on the ham and salad lunch until the following morning because he was unable to eat after the meeting. I thought that perhaps he was working on a new sermon, but sure enough, out it came —Romans 3. I asked him why it was necessary for him to prepare, why he had to fast and pray to such an extent. 'It is more necessary to pray when giving an old sermon, than when giving a new one.' 'But what do you do?' I asked. 'Well,' he told me, 'I pray the sermon over to the Lord point by point. As I do this the Lord impregnates the old sermon with new power. I daren't preach an old sermon without praying the rejuvenating power of the Holy Spirit into my message.'

This is the answer for those of us who use the same outlines. F. W. Boreham, the famous writer said : 'If new sermons are born in my soul, I welcome them and preach them, but do not court them. In the course of your ministry you have prepared and preached sermons which your heart's best blood has been poured in. In a word, they are yourself. Deliver those sermons again and again.'

A soloist uses the same solo; a pianist does not depart from playing the classics, and it did not surprise any of us when at the Royal Albert Hall rally, full to capacity once again, the fifty-fifth time, Tom preached on Romans 3.

There were difficult times when everything fell flat, when we realised we were being tolerated, not supported, and sometimes actively opposed. In one place all the stewards of the church went out into the vestry to count the collection and have a smoke during the sermon. After a ministers' meeting I met Tom looking white and grim. 'What have they done to you?' I asked. 'Have you ever seen a terrier attacking a rat? I was the rat. They hated my message and method, and said so without grace or manners.' If ever a woman doubts if she loves her husband after twenty years, all that is needed is for him to be attacked in this manner.

The liberal-minded minister doesn't believe in missions. The day of mass evangelism is over, he considers, but if his evangelical brethren wish to invite the evangelist, well, it can do no harm, so he puts his name down for the invitation. He dislikes the evangelist personally, but if the others are going to join in, well, he'd better do so because he wants to prevent any sheep-stealing from his flock. He adds his name to the invitation.

The minister that I would call 'the Rev. S. O. Apathetic' always takes the line of least resistance. His congregation is dwindling, and the treasurer is alarmed about the state of the finances. If the mission will help either of these, then as long as he is not actually involved in hard work, he is willing to put his name down. Along with these signatories are men upon whom the evangelist can count, who would cut off their right hand if necessary for him, pray sacrificially, and work a twenty-five-hour day when needed.

Of course, it is hard on the unsuspecting evangelist who hears of this unanimous invitation, and fondly imagines that each church will pull its weight. Meanwhile he prepares himself and prays and comes to the district ready for the fray, only to find that Mr. Apathetic has done nothing—the posters he promised to put up are still lying on his desk, and he has forgotten to announce any of the preparation meetings. The members of his congregation are quite surprised to hear that there is a mission at all.

Mr. Liberal-Minded has grudgingly announced the meetings, but has not closed any of his young people's activities; in fact, when questioned by his own people, he adopted a rather 'go if you dare' attitude.

The Rev. Wolf-in-Sheep's Clothing, now that the invitation has been sent, can remove a little bit of the fleece he was wearing to make a good impression; as the mission proceeds and little happens, he can happily get together with his colleagues and say he knew that it was bound to be a failure.

Tom likened evangelism to warfare. God knew what He was doing when He looked out over Gideon's army of 32,000, and weeded them out stage by stage until he had just the 300 He could trust.

I recently heard a sequel concerning one rally. In my diary it says: 'Talked to two married couples. All four converted that night.' Tom revisited this place.

'May I tell you how you helped to save our church?' asked the local vicar. 'I went to a new church, and it seemed that I had total opposition. Because of my message and the fact that I disapproved of many of the church activities, the entire congregation left me. I had no vicar's warden, no people's warden—nothing. My wife spoke to a small women's group, and from that I arranged a coach party to visit your Mission to Britain rally. Two couples were converted, and came and asked

139

if they could join my church, but they had never been to church, and knew nothing about Christianity, the Bible, or the Prayer Book. I invited one husband to be a vicar's warden, and the other to be a people's warden! The numbers in the congregation crept up, and now with a university in this city, we cannot accommodate the crowds of students who want to come to a church that was nearly closed.'

After eight months Tom felt that it had been, as he put it, 'a thousand times worth while.' He wrote:

'Was it worth it? The answer is emphatically yes, a thousand times worth while. If we had merely held successful meetings, merely interested people, merely excited or entertained vast congregations, or merely inspired churches and individual Christians, I should have serious reservations in giving such a decisive, affirmative reply to the question, but when you have seen at close quarters, as we have done, the most unbelievable way in which God has proved Himself not only faithful, but triumphant, amid all the difficulties and problems that we have confronted in these months, we cannot doubt or deny the fantastic blessing that God has given. He has been glorified by direct, intelligent conversions resulting immediately from the rallies, and apart from anything else the unbelievable number of people who have found Christ through the mission is both its reward and its justification. There is a tremendous satisfaction in being able to say at the end of the mission that the sound of the gospel has gone out into the land; every part of Britain has been able to hear and understand God's peace terms to mankind. The supreme lesson of the mission which has struck me at every turn is that prayer is the key to the entire situation, the lifeline between ourselves and God. To be able to tell each congregation in the mission that throughout the world Christian people are concentrating all their faith and sympathy and prayer on that particular town gives tremendous authority to the declaration of the gospel. To me personally this is the factor which enabled me to sustain the responsibility and strain of preaching night after night for eight months. I have been conscious all along that I am not a lone agent, but the spokesman of a vast body of Christian people whose prayer makes all the difference in the situation —for you.

The way God provided our financial necessities was in keeping with the way our physical and spiritual needs were met. We had no crises or anxiety that distracted Tom from the spiritual burden. In each place we took a collection, and fortunately were not plagued with people who feel it is unspiritual to pass the plate around, and suggest a retiring collection instead. Tom often wondered why it is considered unspiritual for the box to pass the people, but quite in order for people to pass the box! Each night people gave generously—the largest collection proportionately came from Aberdeen!'

We had two anonymous gifts, with upwards of £200 in ancient notes enclosed in a cocoa tin. As we drove from Stratford-on-Avon I asked Tom what was fluttering on the windscreen wiper. It was a cheque for thirty pounds from a woman who had been converted the previous night. In an Irish town one woman had received such help that she rushed home to get a five pound note for the funds; the shilling she had given was inadequate for the blessing received. Steadily as the Lord's people gave, the necessary funds came in, and looking back I am sure that the freedom from financial anxiety was a real factor in Tom's utter dedication to the task resulting in a tremendous harvest.

At the end, those who had travelled on the tour had an informal meal for rejoicing and relaxing, and we did not have ham and salad! There was plenty of fun and reminiscences, quips, and cracks. Tom had a beautifully bound New Testament for each of us, with our initials engraved, with a personally written 'thank you' in each. I wrote an ode recalling many of the lighter moments, and also the heart of the matter. It concluded:

In years to come we'll not forget
These months of labour, toil, and sweat,
Each hour we spent was gladly given
Each day when souls were won for heaven,
Each prayer we prayed, the time we gave
Was something precious, and we have
Memories stored up of wondrous things
As we mount up on eagle's wings.

It is rare that every member of a team is wholly dedicated, carrying their quota of responsibility, but in this mission with Ian Cory as the organiser, the musical and clerical staff were a completely co-ordinated team.

I said to Tom, 'You must not plan anything else for a long time, you must have a rest.'

'Rest?' he said, 'Rest? Whatever for—we have all eternity to rest.'

Although during the mission Tom remained full of energy, when it was over, he was completely exhausted. He told me he was so spent that he almost burst into tears when he had to fill his fountain pen.

Through the kindness of Mr. Stuart Catherwood we went to County Donegal and stayed in his hotel at Rosapenna. Tom had long walks up and down the silver sands beside the sea. Jennifer and I, with some Irish friends played with the 'little white ball', and Tom taught her to drive the car on a lonely stretch of sand.

Walking round the Atlantic Drive, Tom was hitting out with his walking stick—I knew the signs. 'You have a guilty look,' I told him. 'Come on, out with it.' 'I was just thinking ...' I always said 'What with?' in reply—it was an automatic reaction. He went on: 'I saw the newspaper today ... there was a picture of the Queen touring Canada right across the country, and it occurred to me ...' 'I know, don't tell me,' I said. 'Why not a mission to Canada?' 'Got it in one,' he said. 'Go easy,' I told him, 'you must have a rest.' He agreed, and said it was only a thought for *years* ahead in the future. It might have died on him there and then if he had not received a letter, and met a man in the hotel lounge as we returned from our walk. The letter said: 'Dear Tom, I have been reading with much interest about your Mission to Britain, and wondering if you could conduct a similar mission here in Canada.' No sooner had Tom received that letter than a Canadian stepped up to him. 'Excuse me, aren't you Tom Rees? Last time I saw you, you were preaching in British Columbia. It's high time you came back to Canada, the folk there would give you a grand welcome.'

These three events taking place between breakfast and lunch, Tom felt were more than coincidence. After lunch I said, 'Get your stick, and let's go for a walk.' On the sand dunes I said, 'Will you work from Nova Scotia to Victoria, or vice versa?' We were off ...

CHAPTER SEVENTEEN

Mission to Canada

Tom's forties continued to be a time of living to the full. Every day was lived flat out, with no long stretch for re-creating mind or body. The fact that large scale evangelism was temporarily in abeyance did not prevent Tom from visiting the States—New York; Portland, Oregon; Seattle, Chicago, Flushing, Florida, Schenectady, Baltimore, Buffalo, and then on to Canada—Winnipeg and Toronto.

After the Mission to Britain I pleaded with Tom to have a sabbatical year—or six months, or even threee months. He heartily agreed, but I had made an indiscreet remark, and I blame myself for it.

London's City Temple, made famous by the great preacher, Dr. Parker, had been wonderfully restored. The Queen Mother had opened this modern church after its devastation by bombs. Motoring through Devon I casually remarked, 'What a good place the City Temple would be for youth rallies.' This was enough for Tom, who suggested that a series there would be a legitimate pastime during his sabbatical year. Also, he had heard that the musical *The Flower Drum Song* was likely to run on for some time, and he could book the Palace Theatre for Sunday night services in the autumn. These two things came to pass. They were both great series.

As the diary opens for 1960, and when Tom comes to the last of his forties, he writes in a comparatively light-hearted way, in

Setting off in the residential train to the maritime provinces.

The 'impossible' happened; the team was commissioned by recognised heads of all major denominations.

Boarding the plane for a 26,000 mile tour.

Oliver Styles, Tom's friend and colleague.

Our mobile home and office — the Bedford.

contrast to most of the annual comments on January 1st and 2nd. For instance, in 1954 he writes: 'Another year. How many more before I see Him?' 1955 was not much better: 'Another year. I wonder how many more before this may be my last? Spent the day working hard and accomplishing nothing as usual.' The following day, his spiritual birthday, he says: 'I have been a Christian for twenty-eight years, of sorts. I have no spiritual power whatever.' In 1957, on his same spiritual birthday: 'I have been a Christian for exactly thirty years. And very little I have to show for it all. I am ashamed indeed.' In 1959: 'How little I have grown—how little I have done for Him.' But in 1960 he must have had a restful New Year's Eve because he writes, 'I have exactly £75 in the world in cash, but more things money cannot buy, and I trust a little wealth in heaven too.'

In the previous year Tom's father had died and his mother came to live in a bungalow in Frinton. No one could have done more for his mother than Tom. He never failed her; birthdays and anniversaries always brought flowers. Her house, her car, her general welfare and health were his first concern.

When Tom reached his fifties all thoughts of sabbatical years or even days off were quite forgotten. He was gripped with the urge for a Mission to Canada. He had known and loved Canada and the Canadians for many years, having conducted missions in Winnipeg, Victoria, Vancouver, and Toronto. The warm-hearted generosity of Fred Lang and Hugh MacKinnon in Winnipeg was something all of us remember, for that mission was during the time when rations were scarce, and to feed guests at Hildenborough was a problem. Food parcels came in abundance from those generous Canadians. I am constantly reminded of it by the pen on my desk, given to Tom by a brother and sister converted during that mission. The inscription in silver reads, 'Tom Rees—by reason of him much people went away and believed on Jesus.'

Tom went to Canada first of all to get very clear guidance—whether to have a mission at all. It was such a mammoth undertaking that he had to be sure that the plan was of God. Many times he prayed, 'If Thy presence go not with me, carry us not up hence' (Exod. 33:15). Tom learned that to reach the people of Canada with the gospel, it must be done through the recognised denominations. In Britain interdenominational work was not only possible, but successful. In Canada, he was told, 'You'll have to decide whether you are going to have an Anglican mission, and then you will get superb support—The Primate of all Canada is most sympathetic—or whether to go with the United Church [Methodists to us], or Presbyterians or Baptists, but you will never get them all to unite. It's impossible.'

The impossible happened. I wonder if it had ever been known in a large country like Canada, for an evangelist, British or American, to be commissioned for a crusade by the recognised heads of all the major denominations? In February 1961 Tom and his team were commissioned by the Most Rev. Howard H. Clark, Primate of the Anglican Church of Canada; The Rev. Robert Lennox, Moderator of the Presbyterian Church in Canada; The Rt. Rev. Hugh A. McLeod, Moderator of the United Church of Canada; The Rev. Gerald M. Ward, President of the Baptist Federation of Canada, and Commissioner W. Wycliffe Booth, Leader of the Salvation Army in Canada. These men did not merely give mental assent; they gave wholehearted prayerful support. We even had a special message from the Prime Minister of Canada, The Rt. Hon. John G. Diefenbaker, saying, 'No nation can be truly strong, and international and world problems are impossible of solution, unless founded on the eternal principles of Christian faith and witness. The Mission to Canada, bringing together as it does in Christian fellowship members of various Protestant churches in ecumenical unity, is deserving of a welcome in all parts of this country.'

To travel the length and breadth of such an enormous country (it is difficult to believe that when we reach the east of Canada, we are nearer to Britain than to the extreme west of Canada), and to meet the people necessary was a tremendous undertaking. On his preparatory visit Tom was anxious to have a personal interview with the Primate of all Canada, whose home was in Edmonton, 2,000 miles from Toronto where he was staying in the Park Plaza Hotel. He put through a long distance call to the home of the Primate, hoping to talk with him personally, but to his disappointment was told that His Grace had gone away.

'He has broken his journey in Toronto,' said the Primate's secretary, 'and is staying in the Park Plaza Hotel.'

'And so am I,' said Tom in amazement.

He went down two floors in the lift, and had a time of prayer and fellowship with the Primate.

'Be sure to visit the Bishop of Cariboo,' Maurice Wood told Tom before he visited Canada. Tom in his ignorance had imagined Cariboo, where the Bishop lived, was in the suburbs of Vancouver, but looking it up on a map he saw that it was four hundred miles away. Early next morning as he walked into the dining car an Anglican clergyman entered through the opposite door. His face was vaguely familiar to Tom, and the recognition was mutual.

'Excuse me,' asked Tom, 'are you an Anglican minister?'

'Excuse me,' he said, 'is your name Tom Rees? I'm Ralph Dean, I followed your brother Dick at St. Luke's. I used to bring parties of young people to your Royal Albert Hall rallies.'

'And where are you now?' Tom asked him.

'I'm the Bishop of Cariboo,' he replied.

Tom had a friend called Joe in Vancouver who had been helpful in a successful campaign in Victoria's great cathedral. Tom asked Joe if he could arrange a ministers' breakfast to tell them about the proposed mission to Canada. Joe was very disappointed because on the day Tom had chosen to visit Victoria there was a very big service in St. John's Anglican Church, and all the clergy and ministers in the area, and all the civic leaders and people of importance, as well as the general congregation, were gathered there for the centenary in this church to hear the Archbishop preach. The Archbishop heard that Tom was in

Victoria, and invited him to attend the service. Tom arrived expecting to enjoy a busman's holiday, but was sent for by the Archbishop and told he was to read the lesson, and to 'process' in with the bishops. He was placed in a seat of honour. He read the lesson and sat back to be edified by the Archbishop's discourse. He could hardly believe his ears when His Grace said: 'We have a very distinguished visitor from England— I have decided not to preach tonight, but call upon him to give a message worthy of this historic occasion—Mr. Tom Rees.'

I maintain that the Archbishop was unable to resist the temptation of catching a British layman out! But Tom was equal to the occasion. It really was a case of claiming the promise, 'Open thy mouth, and I will fill it.' Tom had been memorising and meditating on Matthew 5, verse 14, 'A city that is set on a hill cannot be hid', and was able to give a talk which, if not worthy of the historic occasion, at least earned Tom the right to speak afterwards to the whole congregation during the refreshments.

'He's coming to Canada soon to conduct a mission, and we're all going to support him,' the Archbishop told them. 'Every one of us, and here he is to tell us about it.'

Afterwards Joe looked at Tom with tears in his eyes.

'I thought I had let you down,' he said, 'but I could never have gathered such a distinguished congregation to hear what you had to say. The Lord has done far better than I could.'

All seemed set for the mission of a lifetime. As we had such denominational support, we felt that more than one voice was needed, and that gifted evangelists from other denominations were necessary, so Tom invited Arthur Rose (the boy we met in Banwell, now an Anglican vicar and a virile evangelist), and Alan Stephens, minister of the Methodist Central Hall, Dagenham (Alan Stephens told me, 'If it hadn't been for Tom, I would not have been a preacher. I went to one of his rallies in Air Force uniform. When Tom was leading the chorus "I'm so glad that He included me" everything came alive.')

When we invited Arthur to join us I watched his wife Daphne's face as it dawned upon her that she would be four to five months alone with their three small children. 'Arthur, you must go,' she said. Alan Stephen's wife, Joy, was just as helpful, and so was Phyllis, the wife of Lex Smith, formerly from Glasgow, but then a Baptist minister in the States. The Rev. Arch LeDrew Gardner came as the Canadian organiser. Elizabeth, the British organiser, together with Joyce Silcox and Claire London, held the fort in Toronto. My work was writing articles and reports, and speaking to numerous women's meetings, while Jennifer at eighteen had great opportunities in youth meetings and high schools.

There was co-operation, there was earnest prayer support; we saw wonderful conversions, but the crushing problem was finance. This took us completely by surprise.

During our business meetings when we had carefully considered the plan of the 26,000-mile trek, visiting over a hundred centres, we felt convinced that although there would be many problems, at least finance would not be one of them. We had experienced the generosity of the large centres, but 'what do they know of Canada who only Winnipeg, Victoria, and Toronto know?' We had experienced the great generosity of those in the States, with their considered sacrificial giving, but did not realise that this was not shared by the rank and file of their neighbours in Canada. The Mission to Britain, marked by the steady giving of British Christians, left Tom's heart and mind free for spiritual warfare. Had the support been like this, the Mission to Canada could have been like a prairie fire.

When Billy Graham visited Britain, literally thousands of people offered their services in a voluntary capacity; businessmen took leave of absence; secretaries worked in the evenings, and hundreds filled envelopes and helped in the necessary chores of a big mission. When we asked for young volunteers from the churches in Canada, they were more than willing to come if they were paid! I must hasten to say that there were people whose generosity was astounding, who gave unremitting help outside the places mentioned, but in many centres it was the rule for the congregation to reach for the smallest coin. In one place where we stayed for the weekend our team conducted over twenty services, quite apart from the Mission to Canada series, without anyone receiving either an honorarium or expenses.

We started the tour with a sense of expectancy and high spirits, with the crises ahead unknown. We had a wonderful Commissioning Service—the men of God who headed the denominations were behind us in earnest prayer and interest. In Newfoundland we had fifty degrees of frost; in the Maritime Provinces we encountered frightening blizzards; in Eastern Canada there were torrential rains; in the prairie, choking dust storms; in Alberta a heat wave (103° in the shade); in British Columbia, floods which compelled us to make a detour into the United States to reach our destination; it was on this last trip that on a precipitous road, a black grizzly bear rolled down a hill right in front of the car, missing it by inches. Tom and his party visited all ten Provinces, preaching in 120 centres. Each day for four months they averaged more than two hundred miles, preaching three times. They never had an accident, a day's illness, or missed a single appointment.

During her Canadian tour the Queen travelled in a specially equipped coach which was coupled to regular trains. By contacting the Vice-President of the national railways we were able to book this coach (not, of course, the royal apartments). It meant that we could travel by car to the outlying centres from the coach, and the office work could be carried on during long journeys. It proved quite an experience having a prayer meeting travelling at a hundred miles an hour.

It was exciting setting off from Toronto on the Bedford coach. We had a warm-hearted send-off from our friends in Toronto. I could not begin to describe all we owe to Stan Izon in particular. He was one of God's miracles. Needing a public relations man, Tom was introduced to Stan who had all the qualities required, business drive, efficiency, enthusiasm, and above all, spiritual vision. He sent out press releases, organised publicity, had a television film made, and was instrumental in bringing numbers of people to the rallies, many of whom found Christ.

By travelling in the royal train some thought we were living a life of luxury, but the novelty soon wore off. To share a tiny room, measuring not more than six feet square for some weeks, made the Bedford not all that it was cracked up to be, particularly when the air conditioner stopped and we lived in a fug, or the hot water failed and we became grubby. On our day off some kind members of the congregation allowed us to have a bath in their house. The static electricity made life a strain; moving around the tiny cabin, if you touched a room mate, a terrific electric shock resulted, so we moved warily like boxers waiting for an opening, and we dared not touch the handle of the door or any metal without gloves. We each had a fan in our cabin, and I had a feather hat which kept becoming irresistibly drawn towards it, and soon my hat looked like a pecked chicken! In a church jumble sale I was able to buy another hat for twenty-five cents. Tom said, 'Now, that's really a nice hat.' I knew he hated the other. When he asked where I got it I said, 'In Toronto.' It's necessary to tell one's husband the truth, but they're often much happier if you don't tell them the whole truth!

When Tom and his party went to Newfoundland they found that the planes were not operating to take them to Bay Roberts for the first assignment. They had missed the only train, so they decided to hire a car and motor three hundred miles. They thought of three hundred miles as quite an easy journey—London to Newcastle—but when the Rev. Arch Gardner heard this, I thought he would hit the roof. It was too late to stop the three men (Tom, Alan Stephens, and Arthur Rose) starting on what might have been a suicide trip. They little knew that they were setting off on a journey of practically uninhabited wastes of ice and snow, in a car not fitted with snow tyres. Early in the journey a truck coming round the corner on the crown of the road pushed them into a ditch. Mercifully they landed in a snowdrift, so were not hurt, but the engine was not improved with snow in it. They kept their spirits up in the early part of the day, but as the time wore on the engine began to falter, and they had not seen a sign of civilisation for miles and miles. They did not know that to be marooned in an ice desert, with a temperature fifty degrees below zero did not mean just an uncomfortable night, but almost certain death. Arch Gardner sounded like a cross between a harassed elderly nanny and a keeper whose inmates have escaped from the asylum! He cheered us up by telling about a member of his congregation who got off the bus half a mile too soon, and after trying to force her way through the snowdrifts, was found dead.

Although there were no telephones, the people at Bay Roberts, who were waiting for them to arrive, had heard of this appalling expedition, and had alerted the mounties to be ready with helicopters to search. The car kept on, sometimes having to be pushed up hills, and always in danger of skidding over the precipitous edge of the road. At 10 p.m. the congregation at Bay Roberts, having been waiting for two and a half hours, decided to leave just as the party pulled up outside the church. They were greeted with cheers, and everyone went back for Tom to conduct a short service.

Among the converts at Amherst, Nova Scotia, was the great-great-granddaughter of Sir Robert Peel who founded the English police force in Victoria's reign. In Dartmouth, across the river from Halifax, there was a delightful Scottish minister who told us that twenty-five of his young people were in the after-meeting, one of them his own son. We had a dignified rally at Ottawa—they hadn't had a mission since General Dobbie had been there seventeen years before—and a splendid hearing. I was surprised that here all the posters had been put *inside* the churches instead of outside. They said if we put them up outside it might look like advertising! Canadians have a horror of appearing to be like Americans, but they could learn a little from the States on the subject of advertising.

We had many opportunities for broadcasting and television programmes. When Jennifer and I went over to Prince Edward Island, the last part of our journey was in a tiny plane, and as I am not a good traveller, Arch Gardner gave me an enormous travel pill. He told me it would make me sleepy, but I hadn't a meeting until 9 p.m. That was all he knew! We were taken straight to a television studio where Jennifer and I were asked to speak on a women's programme in the afternoon. I was in a daze, the pill having taken full effect. I knew little of what happened next, but in the cloakroom I saw my face in the mirror— it was bright orange. I thought this was the effect of the pill, but Jennifer's face was the same. This cosmetic made for a better picture. On one occasion with Tom and Frank Boggs, we hurried straight from the television studio to a restaurant, where I discovered that Tom and Frank had forgotten to wash the paint off their faces.

We had some wonderful times. Alan Stephens was late for lunch after a morning service, so many had stayed behind to find Christ. At Stan Izon's church, when Arthur Rose was preaching, he suddenly felt he should do the totally unorthodox thing, making a public appeal at an Anglican morning service. Thirty people came forward, among them a number of married couples, business and professional people.

The Mission to Canada services continued to give us great encouragement, but as we were approaching Montreal the blow fell. We suddenly realised that owing to the inadequate giving, we were facing a debt of £13,000. We all gave ourselves to prayer. Arch Gardner went to the cathedral for some considerable time; Tom went to a church, and I had a long time of prayer in the launderette! Tom's diary showed his anxiety. He wrote:

'Rose at 7.00 a.m. This is my darkest hour for doubts. The finance burden just crushes me down.' And the next day: 'How I dread coming back to consciousness, when it slowly dawns upon me that the financial situation is not a nightmare, but a fact.'

We realised that humanly speaking we could not hope to meet expenses in spite of economies and the reduced team. At our prayer meeting Arthur Rose reminded the Lord of the clarity of the call, and said, 'We lay this need as a challenge, O Lord, a debt of honour, and we count on Thee to meet our needs.'

We kept in touch with our friends not only throughout Canada, but in Britain as well by a weekly cable. The prayers of our friends at home made more difference than we can ever know to the mission. Looking back through the cables we can see the rise and fall of spiritual temperature; sometimes the cables are triumphant, but often there was a note of desperation. 'Please pray that our faith may be strengthened; that our faith may not fail.' During these dark days we arrived back at Toronto.

Had the Mission to Canada been a series of Torontos, what a mission it would have been, but then our faith would not have been challenged; we would have sailed along, and everything would have been easy. Dr. Nelles Silverthorne, a children's specialist at a local hospital, acting as Toronto secretary, was a great inspiration to us. As a comparatively recent convert, he had an attractive freshness of approach; Dr. William Fitch, a friend of ours in the old days in Scotland, the minister of Knox Presbyterian Church in Toronto, was a great supporter during the campaign, and during the huge rallies in the Varsity Arena.

Back at headquarters with Elizabeth, and Sheila Simpson in the office, we had a council of war about finance. It was obvious that retrenchments would have to be made. We would have to reduce the party for the next loop of the journey to only four men who could travel by car. Alan Stephens and I would return home to tell friends about the mission, and to encourage prayer. After the blow had fallen and Tom accepted it from the Lord, he was wonderfully sustained. The physical hardships of the next part of the trip were like a missionary journey. They travelled as much as three hundred miles a day on dust roads in choking heat to a full programme awaiting them.

Tom describes a typical day's programme.

After early breakfast, we take the road and arrive in a small town about midday. There we go to one of the church halls where the ladies of the church have put on an excellent lunch, giving an opportunity to meet local ministers and the committee. After refreshments we have a brief conference and prayer. My colleagues and I scatter for subsidiary meetings; we go off for a television interview, another a women's rally, and I go to speak to a senior high school. Later we gather in a local movie theatre for a youth rally, where some hundreds of teenagers await us, having come in cars from a radius of a hundred miles. Immediately afterwards we meet the ministers for a conference on local evangelism and winning outsiders for Christ. Every Protestant minister for miles around is present. We speak for twenty minutes, and then go straight into discussion. After a brief time of preparation we go to the evening rally; in eastern Canada these were usually held in churches, but in western Canada they were almost invariably in high schools, auditoriums, or ice rinks. The proportion who attend the rallies in the small town is tremendous. Where the population may be only three thousand, at least twelve hundred will be present.

The lack of manpower doubled the work for the men. Had I been able to take the women's meetings and Jennifer the youth meetings, and Alan Stephens some of the other commitments, it would have lifted the load, but as it was there was never a moment for rest. They visited places where there had never been a mission; some rallies were attended mainly by Red Indians who arrived with hundreds of children dashing up and down the aisles, but still, by the built-in radar system which parents have with their children, they managed to listen and benefit.

I set out from Toronto to return to England with mixed feelings. Originally I had planned to go on to Winnipeg where women's meetings had been arranged, but a strong urge came to go home. I had a premonition that all was not well at home, and so towards the end of April I flew home with Jennifer, and realised how wonderfully the Lord had guided me. My father was very ill, and I was able to be with him for the last week of his life. A number of us were present, including the nurses and the doctor when father looked round and said, 'If I should meet my Maker tonight I will say:

"I want no other argument, I need no other plea.
It is enough that Jesus died, and that He died for me" '

That was the last thing he said. I sat with mother as father's life ended. She was holding in her hands the text from her calendar that day: 'Precious in His sight is the death of His saints.'

The next day I had a telephone call from Fort Churchill, Manitoba, where Tom had been preaching at the Garrison Theatre. He was reassured that I was able to be with mother during the difficult months that followed.

A reporter describing Tom at the Thanksgiving Service at the end of the Mission, having reported the hardships of the tour, the extremes of cold and the extremes of heat, said, 'Yet Mr. Rees's radiant vigour was more pronounced than at the outset.' I could have told the reporter a different story. When Tom returned I did not know whether to describe him as a piece of chewed string or a squeezed orange, but his preaching had been remarkably blessed as was that of Arthur Rose.

Owing to the exceptional generosity of some Canadian Christian friends, and the kindness of supporters in Britain, the financial situation gradually improved, and the gap which at one time had been as wide as £13,000, narrowed until £1,000 was needed.

When we had been back home for some months the accounts of the mission had to be audited. There was one week to go, and still £1,000 outstanding. Tom and I talked it over. We remembered Arthur's prayer and the 'debt of honour'. 'Perhaps this time,' I said, 'it is not His will to meet the need. Maybe we have been presuming on the Lord. Perhaps it's to teach us some new lesson.' Tom was quite willing to consider this. 'Our God Whom we trust is able ... but if not ...' On the other hand he was convinced that the Lord had called him to go; we had had a remarkable time, and he was certain that God would meet his 'debt of honour'. My unspoken thoughts were—well, the Lord will have to hurry; He's only got one week—and I went off to join a houseparty in Ireland.

I was staying at a place called Greystones, where Dr. Paul Rees had been speaking, strange to say, on the subject of finance and prayer. My faith was strengthened, but it was to be strengthened even more that evening when I was called out to the telephone. When I returned my friend, Mrs. Hugh Burrows whispered, 'You look ten years younger, what's happened?' I told her.

A Christian friend, whom Tom had known for a comparatively short time, had taken a great interest in our Canadian venture. Although an invalid, he was widely interested in all kinds of Christian work, and this Wednesday morning he motored over to Frinton. On arrival he enquired about the Mission to Canada.

'How have the finances turned out?' he asked.

Tom said, 'Not so bad.'

'Have you met all your expenses?'

'Not quite.'

'Do you need anything?' asked our friend.

Tom said, 'I expect we will be all right.'

And then the friend said in a forthright manner: 'I'm a businessman, don't beat about the bush with me, Rees. Exactly how much is the deficit on the account?'

'If you want to know exactly,' Tom said, 'one thousand pounds.'

Our friend gave Tom a cheque for that sum. Tom told me when I returned of the characteristic response of our three colleagues—Elizabeth, Frances Hay, and Joyce—Joyce burst into

tears of joy, Frances Hay went upstairs and knelt by her bed
and thanked the Lord, and Elizabeth said, 'Give me the cheque,
I'll take it straight to the bank.'

CHAPTER EIGHTEEN

Interlude

AFTER the Mission to Canada Tom was totally spent. We had booked a little chalet in Gstaad for three weeks in August for a family holiday, and this was one of the happiest holidays of our lives. Justyn was fifteen and Jennifer eighteen, and they took charge of us. Tom and I described ourselves as an oppressed minority, but they realised we were exhausted and needed care. I packed them a picnic lunch each day, and off they went climbing and exploring, while their parents tottered around at home. Tom was so exhausted that he counted it a triumph when he was able to walk by the stream to Saenen, half a mile there, and half a mile back. This caused enormous amusement to the family who walked for miles, climbed steep cliffs, and ran all manner of risks. In the evening I delighted in cooking dinner while they told us all their adventures. Justyn's were full of hair-breadth escapes which we took with a pinch of salt. I had warned Jennifer not to go off on her own to solitary places, but one does relax in Switzerland. She had wandered deep into a wood, and had pushed Justyn off on his own because she wanted to have some time to think and pray over her future.

Although Tom had taken little responsibility with the positive training of his children, his example had made a tremendous impact on them. On their daily outings they walked and climbed alone for some hours because, Jennifer tells me, they found it easier to pray by themselves.

159

One of Jennifer's adventures made me feel cold inside. She suddenly saw in the distance a very horrible-looking man stealthily shadowing her. Jennifer put up a quick prayer and whistled for her dog. She hadn't got a dog, but she whistled loudly and a huge alsatian bounded towards her and stood beside her, so she walked steadily to the edge of the wood, the dog at her heel, then when she got back to civilisation it bounded away and left her. 'That was your guardian angel,' Tom said.

We read aloud to each other, interspersing theological books with an exciting adventure of the French underground. Justyn had just learned to play his guitar, and he and Jennifer sang and harmonised songs like 'Little Donkey' and 'Lucky Old Sun'. It was a time of unalloyed happiness, and the conference that followed with over two hundred people at the Palace Hotel, Wengen was an outstanding spiritual success. We had to start out early on the last day, so Tom said that perhaps we should leave our prayer that morning. Justyn wasn't having any. 'This is the most important time of all,' he said. 'We've got to get up half an hour earlier,' so we meekly did.

Throughout the years of conferences both at Hildenborough and at Frinton we have been wonderfully supported by Mr. and Mrs. Jack Stordy. In one year at Frinton they brought 144 young people in parties, and at Wengen they were with us with three members of their family. The youngest daughter, Joy, had always been a great friend of Tom's: she called in at each conference for a confidential chat about her Scripture Union class at school, and he thoroughly enjoyed talking her problems over with her. At Wengen Justyn and she became friendly, but as their friendship deepened Tom told me this was a great pity. I asked him why. 'Because it's too soon, it'll never last. It would have been so much better if they had got to know one another later,' he said. After her domestic science training Joy went to Birmingham to do first children's nursing, and then to take her S.R.N., and Justyn went to the Westminster hotel school.

Tom told me with amusement that Justyn had asked Mr. Stordy's permission to pay his addresses to Joy. This conven-

Canon Bryan Green and Tom Rees becoming honorary Texan citizens.

Colleagues in twenty-five years hard labour: Joyce Silcox, Frances Hay, and Elizabeth Smith.

Dr. Stephen Offord, co-worker with Tom Rees for many years.

The author's father, A. Sinclair, (right)

Informal discussion in the garden at Frinton.

A. Lindsay Glegg, 'the sanest Christian man I ever met' (*left*); and (*right*) Maurice A. P. Wood, Lord Bishop of Norwich, President of the Hildenborough Evangelical Trust.

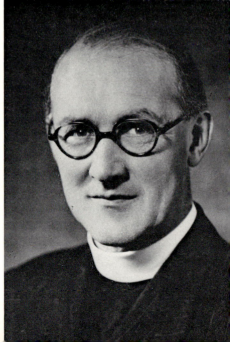

tional behaviour was out of character with modern youth. Not long afterwards, when Justyn had completed his hotel training, and planned to go to the States to complete his commercial flying course, we all went to Wolverhampton for the wedding. In his speech Justyn told us that it was very scriptural that he and Joy should go to the States together to complete his flying, because 'he was finishing his course with Joy!' Although we all thought they were marrying far too young, this was surely God's plan. When God took Tom, Justyn had been married three years, and there is nothing so maturing as marriage for a young man, and to be a father.

I marvel as I trace Tom's life through the years, with the added light from his diary. Increasing exhaustion—'I feel so ill I do not know how I can go on,' and 'I have no strength left'— were accepted as part of his make-up. Others would have retired quietly and settled down, but no sooner had Tom recovered from his exhaustion over Canada than he told me he had two new ambitions.

We were in Switzerland walking to Gsteg. He was carrying the inevitable walking stick, and waving it around as usual. The lease of the Esplanade Hotel had expired, and in order to be freer for evangelistic work, we made Hildenborough Lodge, the house next door, our centre, taking only a few guests in the summer. There was a lull, but strange to say, none of us was happy about it. One might have thought that Miss Hay, after catering for 200, would be glad of a respite, and that Elizabeth, who was free from conferences, would have been delighted to find life easier, but we felt unfulfilled. Even the family felt uneasy about it. Justyn said it seemed wrong to have Christmas all to ourselves instead of sharing it with hundreds of other people. We were all hardened cases, and when Tom told me his ideas, I rallied with enthusiasm.

He did not want another large conference centre; the need for this was adequately met by the Christian holiday week at Butlins, and such centres as Capernwray, but he wanted a small training centre where he could teach people about the opportunities of evangelising by Bible cells. He was concerned with the need and opportunities for groups meeting in private homes, and was planning to write a book about it. This, he felt, was the present way God was working rather than by mass evangelism. He wanted a place where he could have conferences for our own friends, for business and professional people, the kind who would normally only stay at a good class hotel, but who needed the Gospel desperately. The stick emphasised the point!

I asked what else he had in mind. 'I don't suppose *I* could do it,' he said, 'but we need a centre in London where students can go—a hospitality house.' By this time we had reached the little *Gasthaus* in Gsteg, and earned a lunch of fresh trout, Tom's great weakness. We laid the ideas before the Lord in prayer on our walk back to Gstaad. It is always an inspiring experience to pray while looking up at the mountains.

CHAPTER NINETEEN

The New Hildenborough

WE were homeless again, and had been for a few years. We had our bedrooms and ate with our colleagues, but no longer had a place of our own. It was extraordinary to me personally to find that with much less work to do I was unable to write. When I was working fully, organising conferences, the office work and winter evangelism, I was under such pressure that if I paused my brain went on and I could write, orbiting without difficulty. I once wrote five books in one month, all of which are still in print, but once we had slowed down I could not write a word. Mother told me she had never seen me looking so well. I agreed with Tom that the things we were doing—the Palace Theatre service, the City Temple rallies, Swiss conferences, and endless trips to Bible cells from Lands End and back—were not what we were in the world for, and I was not here to live in healthy Frinton feeling well! We were like sailors who have the call of the sea and must go off on fresh voyages.

Suddenly a real dream house came on to our horizon. Combe Lodge, near Bath, built by Sir John Wills, was what my family would call really 'Rees'. It had everything needed for a conference centre; wonderful reception rooms, superb bedrooms, a swimming pool, glorious grounds. It was a bit far from London, but for a holiday centre this was not a disadvantage. Sir John was inclined to let us have it; indeed it was almost settled, and we waited and watched, but only to hear that a training college which had the particular interest of the Duke of Edinburgh was to have it instead. Tom was greatly disappointed.

I had started a book during a holiday in Scotland, but when I returned to Frinton it died on me. It was about a widow of thirty-eight and a charming little girl, Sarah. Jennifer was between her nursery nurse's training and taking a job, and so she and I went to Westerham, and rented an old world cottage with low beams, and set out with stenorette and tapes to finish the book.

When writing a book one tends to get a bit one-track minded, and when Tom said, 'I'll come and stay with you both', I wasn't all that enthusiastic. 'Tom,' I said, 'I love you very much, but I can't orbit when you're around.' However, his birthday was coming up, and we asked him to Westerham on the Friday night, planning his favourite meal.

As I prepared the home-made tomato soup, with salmon, and his favourite lemon pudding, I prayed earnestly, not making a demand, but simply a request, that if God opened up the way for another conference centre, it might have a little corner of our own where I could cook. Tom never liked anything prepacked or frozen, and Jennifer and I hoped he would not know the salmon was out of the deep freeze. I feel relieved too to think that he need never know that the lemon pudding for his birthday, although it was disguised with fresh lemons, really came out of a packet.

We set the table, prepared everything and waited for Tom to arrive. The minutes ticked by. 'The trouble is,' I told Jen, 'he will have a perfect excuse—traffic—diversion—anything, but the plain fact is that he didn't start early enough.' We tried to be patient. I thought of all the instructions I gave at my home-makers' conferences, and the warning monologue I had prepared on 'How to make your husband wish he had married someone else'; the acid tone '*This* is a fine seven o'clock' had to be avoided.

'Don't all shout at me, I can explain,' Tom said when he arrived. I looked at the dried up salmon. 'The excuse had better be good.' 'It is,' he said. 'Wait until I tell you.' We made him eat first, and with the lemon pudding slipping down comfortably and coffee to follow, Tom relaxed. I said, 'There's a birthday card for you—open it, and then give us your "excuse".' The card was from Miss Hay, who always finds appropriate and sometimes offensive birthday cards like 'You do grow old with grace' and inside it says 'Grace is 90'. This one said, 'To the world's best boss,' and inside, 'From the world's most diplomatic employee.' Then she wrote, 'May the Lord give you a Combe Lodge, but near London.' 'Well, well,' said Tom, 'isn't that strange. I think that's just what He has done.'

That morning while having his hair cut he had seen in *Country Life* a house advertised in Otford Hills five miles from Sevenoaks, built by Sir Oliver Lyle of sugar refinery fame. It was a fabulous place with a superb view over rolling hills, surrounded by trees and fields, only it was to be auctioned. 'I think this is it,' said Tom, and he hadn't said that since 1945.

To make a long story short we came, saw, and were conquered, and a little farmhouse only five minutes' walk away, just asking for the Rees family to live in, made things quite perfect. The trouble was we had no time to call a Business Executive meeting if we were to make an offer before the auction. We went and prayed with our three colleagues, Miss Hay, Elizabeth, and Joyce, and were so convinced that this was the Lord's will, we made an offer that we knew would be accepted. The offer was made in our own name, and the next morning we found ourselves quite considerable landowners!

Over the years we had learnt that the Lord provides in things both great and small. Completely without our seeking we were approached by a friend who first of all offered us a £20,000 loan free of interest, and then subsequently made it a gift. Offers of help poured in from people who had attended previous conferences. From Ireland we had gifts of blankets, from Wolverhampton cutlery, and generous financial gifts made it possible for the new Hildenborough to be opened.

It wasn't all plain sailing. We had to work very hard and

remind ourselves about the cattle upon a thousand hills belonging to the Lord, and if ever we forgot the cattle and fear crept in, we drew cheques upon the bank of memory. Very soon Shorehill House became Hildenborough Hall, a house of remarkable beauty, built regardless of expense by a man who could have his rooms panelled, and his furniture fitted, putting up leaded embossed pipes, without estimates or consideration.

While the feverish preparation was in progress another of Tom's ideas was carried into operation. Because we had no summer conferences during 1963, Tom conceived the idea of renting a large hotel in Switzerland with accommodation for 220, staffing it ourselves, and arranging conferences for six weeks. The Palace Hotel, Murren, was not used in the summer, being a winter sports centre. When Tom told Miss Hay the idea, she gasped with horror and asked who was going to manage it. Tom said, 'You,' and Miss Hay said, 'I go not,' but went. We decided to staff it with university students from Britain. We chose a staff of about thirty, most of whom had no previous experience of hotel work, but all of whom had energy, brains, and practical ability. Graeme Thomson, from Queen's, Belfast, who was taking his finals, was the head waiter, and other waiters and waitresses included several B.A.s, a nuclear physicist, and Justyn.

All the staff were determined that the organisation would be superb. It was the staff themselves who decided that everyone should be called 'Sir' or 'Madam', even small boys of fourteen, including close relatives! It was here that Justyn started a guitar group, formed from his fellow workers, and every night hot numbers were rendered as the young people partook of refreshments in the Inferno Bar—('Inferno' being the name of a ski run, no connection with any other place of the same name!) As Tom had left the slum camp with tent pegs scrubbed, so when we left the Palace Hotel, Murren, the owner said that never had it been cleaner.

We returned from Switzerland to have a home of our own at last. The little farmhouse was being prepared for a home, the first for all four of us. I was excited about tea chests of wedding presents that hadn't seen the light of day for eighteen years. While in Murren Tom and I had a day off on our wedding anniversary. I was sure he was going to slash about with his walking stick, planning not evangelism for once, but colour schemes in the kitchen, carpets and furniture. Before we set out I turned to my regular Bible portion, and saw a word of warning in Amos, 'Woe unto them that are at ease in Zion.' The battle was still on, and I prayed that the farmhouse would be a place where we would refresh ourselves for further warfare.

We planned the colours of the tiles, but were so busy getting the conference centre opened, we had to accept the fact that the builders put the black cloakroom tiles in the green kitchen, and the green tiles in the cloakroom!

When our desire for so long was about to be realised I suddenly discovered that my heartbeat had become irregular. Just as I wanted to be at my best in planning the centre and organising our home, I found myself panting like a fish on a slab, and had to spend most of the winter with my feet up. I recovered sufficiently to go to Switzerland with Tom for our winter sports party, but went with an undercurrent of anxiety, for the specialist, after organising an electro-cardiogram, said that when I returned there must be further tests. Having a vivid imagination has advantages and disadvantages. During the days that followed I was convinced that I would have to undergo a major operation. I knew my heart would not stand up to it. Tom commented in his diary, 'As usual Jean thinks she has cancer,' but he was most kind and sympathetic. When we went for little walks it was not to plan evangelism, or even the new home, but to plan a delightful eventide life for me, as I was convinced that if I recovered from my operation, I would be a permanent invalid. In my bedroom would be a low desk and a comfortable chair that would tip up, a dictating machine, and a portable radio. People would visit me for spiritual help, I would write letters, and read the books I had never had time for. It sounded so attractive that Tom told me I had all the luck. Fortunately, none of the tests necessitated such a quiet life.

Miss Hay had a major operation, and by the time the new house was opened, she and I were tottering round together wishing we were twenty years younger, but glad of the experience of nearly as many years in conference work.

After a series of garden parties in July, the conference centre was launched. Many of the Murren students were among the first helpers, and Tom and I found it a tremendous support to have our own family working at the conference centre that summer season. Justyn and the Peacemakers' group sang each evening in the coffee bar; Jennifer and Tony organised games, excursions and walks.

When we found Jennifer and Justyn working so effectively for God Tom said to me, 'I can't think how it happened, we must have done *something* right.'

CHAPTER TWENTY

A Home at Last

AN evangelist is someone who precipitates a spiritual crisis in the life of another. This does not have to be through public preaching, although of course if people will listen, this is possibly the most effective and powerful method. Tom constantly found that God still spoke by 'the foolishness of preaching'. But there were other ways of preaching beside the mass meeting with singing, an address, and an appeal.

Tom revised his phraseology, not consciously, but because he kept in touch with people. He 'sat where they sat', and realised that in speaking to the man in the street—whether the street was the board room, the office, or the factory—he must use their language. Once he talked about being saved, and continued to do so in a limited way, but later he talked more of committing our lives to Christ. He found the word 'believing' was misunderstood, but he still talked of being born again. Strange to say that is understood even by those who have never read St. John's Gospel chapter 3.

Tom had coffee with the wife of a naval commander who had been brought to a lecture when his subject was the Deity of Christ. Tom told her that she needed to be born again; to have a totally new kind of life; in short, to take Christ into her life, to become a Christian—Christ in. That night she knelt by her bed and almost without saying anything she was conscious of being a new person. The next morning she rang the wife of the army officer who had brought her to the lecture. 'My dear,' she said, 'I must come and see you. I think I've been saved. I don't know what it is, but a girl I knew twenty years ago said she was saved, and I've got what she had. Will you tell me what it is?'

Tom had arranged a series of lectures in the London Hilton hotel each Sunday evening for nine weeks, with the title 'The Christian Faith in a Contemporary World'. Tom spoke himself on basic Christian truths and invited other speakers, such as Professor Robert Boyd, the expert in space; the Rev. John Taylor, Major William Batt, and the Rev. John Stott. Three hundred people came by special invitation, and afterwards sat around over coffee.

Tom faced the fact that only five per cent of London's population go to church, and that far less would go to an evangelistic rally; therefore he used his ingenuity and spiritual common sense to reach those who were genuinely searching. Going out to the highways and hedges for him involved going to the Hilton. Week by week numbers increased, particularly of men, who preferred to have their evangelism neat without the trimmings of a service.

One Q.C. was invited by a friend; he read the programme, showed it to his wife, and said, 'We'll go to the whole course, we need it.' During the weeks that followed his wife became a committed Christian, and that Christmas, together with their two daughters who were educated with Princess Anne, they came to our houseparty. The Q.C. had never enjoyed a Christmas so much, and opened his heart to Christ. Two days later, staying alone in his thatched holiday cottage, he was burned to death.

A Christian doctor wrote to Tom refusing to help because he felt the gospel should be for all, and that this was not a New Testament method. Tom saw him later, and asked about his practice. Did he have a private practice, or was it all National Health? He admitted to having a large private practice. 'But why do you do this?' Tom asked. 'Isn't it pandering to snobbish instincts?' The doctor explained that there were better-off patients who wanted specialised attention. Tom explained there were people who needed spiritual healing, who would not go to a vast rally and hear a speaker who might want them to 'get up out of their seats . . .'

On another occasion Tom organised a series of lectures in the Royal Festival Hall entitled 'Science and Religion', when eminent men of letters spoke to increasing interested audiences.

The emphasis in evangelism has altered, with the increase not only of home groups, but coffee mornings, lunches and dinners. It is much more satisfactory if, instead of being instructors, Christians become spiritual parents who pray and care for their contact, like spiritually pregnant people taking them to coffee mornings (like a clinic), and finally perhaps to the spiritual maternity hospital, i.e. the special evangelistic effort. There is less falling away afterwards. As St. Paul said, 'Ye have ten thousand instructors, but only one father.' Tom became convinced that mass evangelism was disappearing, and that churches were becoming places for formal occasions.

He wrote in 1965: 'One of the most exciting things in the spiritual realm taking place in the British Isles today is the amazing growth of home groups, meetings for prayer and Bible study. This movement is not of man, but of God, having its roots deep in the New Testament. All over the country from Lands End to John o'Groats, from Londonderry to Dover, in city and countryside alike, men and women, young and old, are meeting regularly in private homes to study the Bible, to encourage one another in the things of God.'

Tom saw the swing from large-scale evangelism, where nothing succeeded unless there was a complete pack-out, to today when the battle is hand-to-hand fighting, with Christians leading people to Christ themselves, rather than depending upon the vicar, or the evangelist drawing in the net.

Tom's book *Break-Through*, a comprehensive manual about home Bible cells and outreach continues its work on both sides of the Atlantic, so the effort of producing a book in the midst of a hectic life was not wasted.

171

There is always a desire in the heart of an evangelist for a mission of the old-fashioned variety, and when Tom received invitations, in spite of his conviction that large-scale evangelism was out, his whole soul responded. I said one day, 'What's this I read in the Christian press about you taking two missions next year?' He looked guilty and admitted he knew I wouldn't approve, so he did it by stealth!

He had arranged to have two united missions. One was in a district in a large city; the churches were all uniting, he said; and the other was in the Irish city of Kilkeel where the four ministers there were all quite at one with the mission. I said bluntly that I would believe it when I saw it, and told Tom that I thought he was wasting his time. The only possible way to have any successful mission was to prepare it with our own committee, and not to rely totally on local help. Once bitten, twice shy. I could write a book about such missions. We argued happily about this; it was always very stimulating. One of the things I miss tremendously is having someone with whom I can argue without rancour, and where even a row becomes a joke. However, in this case I was so wrong and so right.

The mission at Kilkeel, led by Alan Flavelle who became a Christian when Tom was in Lurgan, was a never-to-be-forgotten experience—more than successful evangelism; it had about it a breath of revival, but the other mission was exactly what I had expected. In Kilkeel, where the mountains of Mourne sweep down to the sea, there were four churches where the ministers not only believed in evangelism, but believed in the particular evangelist who came, who realised that the mission was a warfare, and that they were involved in total war. From the very beginning Tom knew that he had the wind behind him. It was like putting back the clock twenty years. It is quite exciting to look at his diary. There was obviously a real sense of conviction of sin, and God moving among the people there. At the early morning prayer meetings there were no flowery prayers, but praises to the point—'Thank you for saving my husband, for saving our whole family, for saving my brother

172

or my sister,' and earnest prayer asking the Lord to bring salvation to definite people. 'Was up until the small hours of the morning leading people to Christ,' says the diary, 'then until after midnight for someone who had been seeking Christ for many years.'

We soon realised that there was not the slightest danger of our being at ease in Zion where Shorehill Farm was concerned. Looking back I wonder if it was worth while. It cost a great deal of money, but this in itself was a gift from God. For a number of years Tom and I had had a friendly argument. To be happily married does not mean that you should think the same. Tom wrote *Money Talks* and stated plainly that in his opinion income should be tithed gross and not net. I did not agree. I said I was qute willing to tithe what I received. I instanced super-tax payers who might only get sixpence in the pound, but Tom said, 'You're not paying super-tax, and when you do it will be time enough to worry about it. In the meantime I think you should tithe gross, but it's not my business.'

In his book Tom tells of people who resisted tithing, but when they did so, they subsequently prospered. One day I said to Tom, 'I give up, I see the point. I'm going to tithe gross.' It didn't make much difference as far as the amount was concerned, but I believed it was right.

When we rented the Esplanade Hotel in 1954 we needed The Lodge as an annexe, and our colleagues on the business executive quite rightly felt that the Trust was not in a financial position to buy it. Tom and I knew we needed it, so we invested our available capital on it. The next year property slumped in Frinton and the house dropped £2,000 in value. However, we had not bought it as an investment, but for the sake of the work. Just before we planned to move to Shorehill House, a small portion of The Esplanade at Frinton was scheduled for flat development, and our house became three times its original value, enabling us to buy our home, Shorehill Farm. God is no man's debtor.

It was worth having the house for Jennifer and Justyn. Justyn said one supper time, 'A wonderful thing happened to me this evening. Someone said, "Where are you going?", and I said, "I'm going home." It's the first time I have ever been able to say that in my life.'

We soon found that the joy of having a home was not so that the Reeses could have a happy little exclusive huddle on their own, but to see how many we could fit in on camp beds, sofas, and mattresses on the floor. 'Is it all right if the Peacemakers stay overnight?' Justyn would ask. 'We're practising tomorrow.' We grew quite accustomed to entering the front door of the Farm, and falling over amplifiers, guitars, and drums. During one of their practices they composed their signature tune 'Some Folks Search for Peace'. The house reverberated with sounds of rhythm. I remember Tom coming along from his busy work at the Hall, hoping for a little rest. As he put his head round the door the sound hit him. He asked, 'What's going on?' 'Some folks search for peace,' I answered. 'Not here they don't,' said Tom, and went back to the comparative calm of the conference centre.

It was hard for Tom. He had not grown up with a family around him, and was inclined to run the home like the conference centre. It was quite a time before I managed to restrain him from putting up little notices in the home as well as in the centre. I came home and found a little note about the front door being kept shut, and a few other suggestions about how the bathroom and toilet should be left. On a large piece of paper with a red felt pen that must have scorched the paper I wrote him a note: 'Don't ever put up a notice again in this house— this is a home, not a conference centre.' This became quite a joke between us, and I pacified Tom by saying the day would come when he and I would live quietly together in peaceful bliss.

The most important time to have a house is when the family are courting, and soon Jen and Tony, and Justyn and Joy, were 'going steady'. For Jennifer and Tony there were wedding preparations. They were both interested in antiques, and Tom promised to give them an antique Welsh dresser as a wedding present. Together they scoured the country, and attended auction sales, becoming more and more knowledgeable. Furnishing on a shoestring involved buying things that were going for a song, upholstering and restoring them. Tom did not retaliate by putting up a red notice saying 'This is a home not a furniture repository and upholstery factory' as he might well have done.

I went to an auction with Jennifer, and following a hunch she bid for an ungainly black screen which was knocked down to her for five shillings. She was offered five pounds before she left the sale room, but brought it back to find it was gold on vellum. The Victoria and Albert Museum declared it to be the oldest of its kind in England dating to before the first Queen Elizabeth. Tom's wedding present of a Welsh dresser was purchased, and clever shopping enabled the cheque also to run to a genuine James I table.

Soon after they were married, Jen and Tony invited Tom to Sarratt where they lived, for a weekend of meetings. On the Saturday night all the furniture was taken out excepting the Welsh dresser, the screen, and the table, and by seating the guests on stacking chairs sixty were squeezed in. Many were friends interested in antiques. Tom spoke on 'I was an agnostic'. On Sunday evening the stacking chairs were taken out, and nearly a hundred young people sat on the floor and stairs.

CHAPTER TWENTY-ONE

The Closing Years

I HAVE travelled down the corridors of memory through forty-one years of diaries, memories kept green by tears, lit with the sunlight of laughter, often with the misery of what might have been, and inevitable heart searching. Could I have done more, acted differently, or done anything to prevent such a life being cut off when other men were in their prime? Tom lived to the full. There is no gap in his spiritual history. The world, the flesh, the devil seem to have made little headway with Tom.

In his diaries there is no unkind word or criticism concerning any person, colleague or critic, friend or relative. They begin with a struggle to pray, and reflect the deepest desires of his heart in seeking after God. The last diaries still show conflict but never in seeking to pray. The Tom of 1970 had learned the lessons the nineteen-year-old Tom had sought.

Many who only knew Tom as a preacher were surprised to know of his ministry in caring for the sick, the bereaved, and the aged. If true religion and undefiled is to visit the fatherless and widows in their affliction (Jas. 1 : 27), then Tom's religion was genuine. He developed an increasing love for people and concern for their troubles and anxieties. Like his Master, when he heard of bereavement and sickness, he was moved with compassion and did something about it.

'He came all the way to see me only ten days after my husband died,' recalls one widow. 'He made the journey specially to see if I was all right.'

176

(*Left*) Jennifer and Tony married at Orford Church. (*Above*) Justyn, Joy, and Esther.

Justyn and Joy with Stephen Motyer at the Coffee Shop.

Tudor barn at Hildenborough Hall, Shorehill.

When Dr. Scroggie's ninety-year-old sister had a stroke, she said immediately, 'Send for Tom Rees,' and he was there within the hour.

'He sat up all night with me the night my husband died. He knew I would be alone and need comfort,' another told me.

For one he arranged the sale of her house and an annuity, and as she was an invalid, found a suitable home for her to live in. Numbers of widows received loving letters each year on the anniversary of their husband's death, and the continued promise of regular prayer. Here is one such letter:

'I want to assure you of my prayers and loving thoughts next Friday. I have not missed one day during the past twelve months giving thanks for your beloved husband, and commending you to the Lord Jesus.'

To another who was ill he wrote: 'Ever since your operation I have prayed for you each morning by name, asking God to lay His hand upon you, and give you an ever-growing sense of His Presence.'

I visited an invalid a day or so ago who looked really bleak. 'I was going to ask Mr. Rees what to do with my property,' she said. 'He'll never come again. He used to say "how are *you*" and he wanted to know the answer. It was like ... the Lord Himself coming into the room.' Then she looked at me and said, 'I suppose you miss him too.' Only Tom's secretary, Joyce Silcox, knew of the flowers that were sent on anniversary days, the letters of comfort and counsel, and the way in which the Lord was able to take the loaves and fishes of Tom's ordinary life and multiply them because they were freely given.

I am allowed to quote the following letter: 'Some years ago after I first came to know Tom Rees I grievously sinned against my Lord and society, and as a result I was sent to prison for three years. It was then that I came to know something of the extent of the practical outworking of Tom Rees's faith. He constantly kept in touch with me, even coming a considerable journey in order to visit and minister to me. During a preaching tour in Canada he used his influence with the Archbishop of

British Columbia to find me employment. His letter on my return home was characteristic—"Remember, that what God forgives, God forgets. There's a blank in His memory concerning all our sin. What is more, the children of God have that same convenient memory. The past three years must be completely forgotten by us all." '

During an informal weekend conference, Major William Batt, Deputy Lieutenant of Norfolk, told us: 'I learned a tremendous lot from Tom, and there's no man in England that I miss more, not because we met often, but because he was a man of God that one respected and loved. I think one of the first times I met him was at the Albert Hall, and I thought then this man is everything I don't like. But I thought to myself—here are 10,000 people off the streets of London, right out of their own environment, and here was Tom singing with them, and by the time he got up to speak they were so relaxed— they felt that here was someone they knew. The last time Tom and I were together he came and conducted an evangelistic crusade for us, it was quite different. I don't think I have ever in my life sat and listened to someone who was so utterly selfless, and so utterly gracious.'

Another writes: 'I cannot think of any evangelical leader in this country who combined so many gifts, together with such energy and vision.'

These are only opinions, and would certainly have astounded Tom.

More letters disclose the man he had become.

'... We never made a big decision without his counsel. In the Christian world everyone wondered what Tom Rees would think about any crisis.'

Billy Graham wrote to me that when he was considering coming to Earls Court, and was determined to say 'no', he asked Tom to meet him at the boat at Southampton, and drive up to London with him to discuss the matter.

'Tom told me,' he said, 'that he thought it was right for me to come. It was twelve years after Harringay, and the time was ripe, and when he said "come", I knew that this was the right advice.'

A business man writes: 'I always remember Tom for his great kindness when I was down. He encouraged me after my business had failed. I will miss his counsel greatly.'

'I cannot understand it,' said the father of two Hildenborough teenagers. 'When I was a teenager Tom Rees helped and inspired me, but although I have grown older, and become a father, Tom Rees seems to have remained the same age, and can help my teenagers.'

In Tom's last years, in an increasing measure he was like Abraham's servant: 'I being in the way, the Lord led me.' God brought people across Tom's path because he was ready to use every opportunity. He went out to dinner and afterwards asked me, 'Have you ever heard of a golfer called John Jacobs? I went to dinner with him last night.' 'Have I ever heard of John Jacobs?' I replied. 'I have read his books, heard him on television, and when Jennifer was Essex Girl Golf Champion she was invited to train in John Jacobs' school to play against the American team.' Tom told me about the dinner party where he was introduced to John, who was relieved to hear Tom wasn't a golfer. 'I don't want to talk about golf,' he said, 'I want to know how to become a real Christian.' He explained that his wife, from being only an outward Christian, had become a person with a real vital faith. 'I used to pray "Please God make me a good Christian." Now I pray "Please God, show me how to become a Christian."' Before he left in the early hours of the morning Tom showed John just that. 'My wife and I were deeply touched at Tom's memorial service by the joy and assurance seen all around us,' John told me, 'I would like you to know that Tom helped me to find the same assurance in getting through to me that Jesus really did die for all men, and that included me.'

A business man who joined our Swiss party wrote: 'Meeting him was a turning point in my life, and as a result I became a convinced Christian. Tom was not only able to preach to thousands, but also to help people individually. I must confess I have always tended to have an aversion to mass evangelism. What did appeal to me about Tom was that despite the enormous extent of the calls on his time and energy, he found time to see people individually, and to give them the feeling that they mattered to him. I think the important point about Tom was that he was a merry Christian. He cut through all the useless trimmings of religion, and confined himself to the essentials with enthusiasm, deep knowledge and, most lovable quality, a delicious sense of fun.'

The year Jennifer was married was a testing time. When she left home it was like a day when the sun went in, but this was not the only cloud on our horizon. The summer conferences were difficult. In the previous three summers Tony had been the chief organiser, and Jennifer had helped. We suddenly felt old and realised that something was wrong with Tom's health. He became exhausted and blacked out each afternoon, and although he said little about it, he arranged to have a complete medical check-up. He had been invited to speak at the World Congress on Evangelism in Berlin organised by Billy Graham, but was unable to do so. I now know that he thought he had leukaemia or some serious blood disease, but beyond cancelling the Berlin conference he continued working at the same pressure.

In his diary in October 1966 he puts in capitals, 'I AM DIABETIC.' In a sense there was relief that it was no worse, but I was horrified. However, he soon became accustomed to arranging a special diet, and when less than a year later I too became diabetic, we took it quite light-heartedly! But from then on life was a fight, sometimes a losing battle. We understood each other, and knew the horror of diabetic exhaustion, the all-time low which for Tom was 3 p.m., and for me 7 p.m. We called it going over to capital when we had spent our physical income. We should, of course, have retired then—or should we? God sent a wonderful provision in the form of a girl from Ireland called Roberta Gribben. She had been my secretary for a year, but now told me she considered we needed looking after. As her father was diabetic, and her mother had a bad heart, she knew all the answers. She moved into our home as housekeeper/secretary, and I can never thank God enough for giving us someone in Tom's last five years who made our home so serene, and made it possible for us to continue our work.

We did not ease up. I had a tour with Roberta to the United States to speak at ladies' lunches, and returned to launch a large number of these in Britain. The following November Tom organised a mission in Coleraine, County Londonderry, one of the most fruitful missions we had held for many years. This time Tom took a team of evangelists including Major Batt, Tom Butler, a well-known Methodist, Roger Forster, Brigadier Francis Tarrant, the Rev. Ian Fisher, the Rev Robert McGhee, and Edward Smith. Each church had its own mission with its own missioner. Tom's part was to co-ordinate, speak at the ministers' breakfast, organise the prayer meetings, and speak from time to time at the different centres.

As we motored to Larne for the car ferry I said to Tom, 'If this mission follows the usual pattern of missions organised by local churches, it's the last one I will ever attend.' 'What do you mean?' he asked. I reminded him of missions where ministers who had no faith in the mission, and made no preparation, came and then asked for the names of those to follow up afterwards. I was mistaken. I have never known a place where our suggestions for preparation and organisation were so wonderfully carried out as in Coleraine. Martin Garner, the secretary, attended to the finest detail. All church activities had been cancelled. Dr. George Humphreys, headmaster of the Coleraine Academical Institute, a school of 1,200 boys, together with the headmistress of the girls' school, even postponed rugby matches and hockey teas, and arranged that their boarders could attend the 7 a.m. prayer meeting without losing their breakfast! As for the ministers and their wives, I did not know such people existed. As a result the harvest was wonderful. Coming back to the manse where we were staying was like returning to a spiritual labour ward; there were people in every room waiting to be converted. By special Government permission a postmark with the New Life emblem—the cross with sprouting leaves, was sent on all letters, and went all over the world.

Occasionally, Tom and I discussed our physical limitations. One Christmas he had 'flu, and as he lay in bed quite relaxed I said, 'Can't you think of a really nice illness you could have? You're so lovely when you're ill!' It was true. Instead of what I call his 'abstract' look, the 'I'll-have-to-go-back-to-work-almost-immediately face' he kept saying, 'Don't hurry away—sit down and talk,' and we'd have cosy cups of coffee.

One of Tom's uncles, a good-looking, vigorous man, had a stroke, and the next day he was a helpless invalid. This was Tom's horror. 'I want to go out in full flight like Fred Mitchell of the China Inland Mission,' he said. We discussed how to invest our energies, whether we should be what I called battery or free range hens; battery hens produce a record number of eggs in a year, free range hens last longer but produce less! Should we go on at full pressure, and wear out rather than rust out? Tom deliberately opted to wear out, and although I began to flag and tried to go slow, it went against the grain.

Even before Tom was pronounced a diabetic he had suffered from exhaustion almost beyond bearing, but he took this as the normal way of life. Paul had his thorn in the flesh and lived to be Paul, the aged, so Tom's spirit and imagination rose above his physical disabilities.

He was not old. It is the characteristic of old men to dream dreams, but he saw visions. It was during this time that Tom inevitably got a new idea, a spiritual vision. It was twenty-five years after his debut in the Central Hall, Westminster when the Mission 'This is the Victory' took London by storm. He had no desire whatever to repeat the mission, but something different was born in his mind and heart. His concern about the decline of his own country became an obsession in the best sense of the word. He felt that he must somehow warn the nation of the terrible danger it was in. So the idea of a national mission grew. The Central Hall, Westminster was free for the month of September 1970, so Tom made a preliminary booking, and started planning. He invited George Polson, the eminent Q.C., to paint a picture of Britain today—vice, divorce, teenage pre-marriage pregnancy, drug addiction, crime and violence. He invited Malcolm Muggeridge to speak on the permissive society; and Cliff Richard, who not only captured the minds and imagination of teenagers, but had a message and a conviction to put over. He invited scientists as well as preachers, with face-to-face interviews and confrontations, rather than direct preaching. The final meeting would be in St. Paul's Cathedral.

It was planned that on the first day of the series 'Time for Truth' the original beacons of 1588 should be fired from Plymouth to London to emphasise that Britain was once again in mortal danger.

He tried to obtain the help of several notable organisers, but he was not successful, so he shouldered the whole load himself, with the aid of many excellent committees. I have heard it said that the organising and planning of 'Time for Truth' was too much for Tom and caused his early homecall, but I do not think this is so. He would always have been organising something else, and would inevitably have been called Home during some fresh enterprise. 'Time for Truth' was just such another.

The idea gripped Tom, but for once I was a slow starter. For the first time in our lives, when he had an idea and wanted to talk it out, my response was lukewarm. Secretly I just could not face it. I knew how ill we both were. I imagined him preaching each night for three weeks, and I knew that he would have to do the organising and inspiring. However, when Tom went off to Winnipeg I suddenly got the vision too. I wrote him a letter, and you can imagine how I felt when I found it in his diary on April 20th, the day he died. He had kept it for over a year, and I will always be so glad I sent it. I wrote:

My dearest—What a dreadful helpmeet I am for you with such dreary lack of faith and so feeble. Today I suddenly had returning strength, and instead of breaking out into a sweat at the thought of the future, I felt an urge and a challenge. I realised:

1. The devil doesn't like the idea of September 1970.
2. The Lord can give you a Caleb strength; able 'to go out and come in, as it was then'.
3. It is nothing to Him to save by many or by few.

The joy of the Lord is our strength. I had a lovely sense of His presence, and that does help. I woke up feeling that my strength was restored, so forgive me as your colleague for being faithless about next year. If you have the call for it, then He will carry us through as in September 1945, the Mission to Britain, and all other things between.

Joy rushed to her father-in-law with enormous excitement. 'I must tell you,' she said. 'It's been confirmed.'

'Who's been confirmed?' he asked.

'The baby,' said Joy. 'I've just heard from the doctor, it's been confirmed.'

'Well, I think that's far too young,' said Tom, but joined us at the Farm in a cup of his special coffee to rejoice in Justyn and Joy's great expectation.

It was three years since Justyn had left home. Having trained as a commercial pilot, worked at Canadian Keswick, had experience in building, he decided that Joy and he should have six months' vacation in England so that the baby (now confirmed) could be born.

The last thing Justyn wanted was to run Hildenborough Hall. Tom and I had made it clear from his earliest days that we had no desire for him to follow in our footsteps. The burden a young man carries when he knows that he must take on his father's

184

practice or business is one no parent should ask his son to carry.

'It is total commitment,' I warned Justyn; 'you have to be prepared to give everything if you are to achieve spiritual success, and nothing else is worth having.' Justyn obtained his hotel management diploma, and then every kind of flying certificate.

He came with an open mind to help us on the conference centre as a holiday occupation, but suddenly he became enthused with the potential of Hildenborough Hall for his own generation. Ideas surged in his mind. He made notes and drew plans, and practically dragged his father into Knole Park. Together they walked, and as Tom slashed out with his walking stick, he listened to ideas to which his whole mind and soul responded.

Justyn was concerned about the young men and women who were not yet down-and-out; who were not yet 'hooked', but who had no purpose in life.

'We need a place where young people can come with their problems and find the truth,' he said. 'You must have more accommodation, a tape library, counsellors to answer questions; you must make Hildenborough available to people who can't book up beforehand, but who need to come urgently. You need family units and a large new conference hall.' Justyn pulled the plans from his pocket and spread them out on a fallen tree.

'Not quite so much of the "you",' Tom told him. 'If this is to be done, *you* must do it. I agree with you, it rings a bell with me, but I cannot do it.' Tom told Justyn that his health was such that he was only just managing to cope, and that soon he would need to retire.

It was a great surprise to Justyn. He had thought of father as timeless, and the idea of his retiring was astonishing. 'Yes,' he said, 'I suppose it's time you stopped doing three jobs, and just did one.' They prayed and went into meticulous details of all that had to be done. The problem was, when? Should Justyn stay in Britain and after the September 'Time for Truth' meetings gradually take over, or should he go away, take up a flying job for a time, and in three years return?

After the new baby was born, we had a family council at Jennifer and Tony's house. There was almost a patriarchal atmosphere. Jennifer and Tony's children had said goodnight to grandfather, but not before he had secretly slipped some sweets into their hands in a manner quite against the Larcombe rules. There was Sarah ('Thou shalt call her name Sarah, and I will bless her'—Gen. 17:15); Justyn Elliott (called Elliott after Tony's great-great-Aunt Charlotte Elliott who wrote the hymn 'Just as I am'), and baby Esther in the carry cot (Esther who 'obtained favour in the sight of all them that looked upon her'—Esther 2:15).

We sat around and I said with satisfaction, having at last got everyone together, 'Let's talk it over.' Tom said, 'No, let's have some prayer first.' I felt that was good-bye to our discussion because I knew what Tom and Justyn were once they started praying! Over an hour and a half later, having laid the future before the Lord from every angle, and consulted the heavenly headquarters, Tom said, 'Now, we'll each pray for the one who is sitting next to us. I'll pray for Justyn, he'll pray for Tony, and so on.' Tom poured out his heart to God for his son. It was like David commending Solomon—'Be strong and of good courage, and do it: fear not, for the Lord God, even my God, will be with thee'—1 Chr. 28:20. Then we talked.

Tom asked, 'Are you quite sure, Justyn, that you want to leave flying and eventually run the conference centre?' Justyn said that he found flying most exciting, but the work at Hildenborough, and the opportunity of reaching the young people there was even more exciting. When it was suggested that Justyn should come and assist Tom, I was very strongly against this. 'You can't have two Mr. Reeses,' I said. 'You are far too strong-minded, and you both have your own ideas.' It was finally decided that Justyn should go back to Canada and gain further experience, and then in three years' time return to carry out the plans that both Tom and Justyn had agreed were of God.

Three years! I did not utter my secret thoughts. I was convinced I would not live for three years at the present pressure of life; three years of conference and evangelistic work—three long years before release. Tom's spirit shone through his physical weakness, deceiving anyone but those who were very close.

Justyn flew back to Canada on February 17th, 1970, two months before his father died. Tom wrote in his diary, 'God give me strength.'

It is less than a year ago, and we are together again, Justyn and Joy, Tony and Jennifer and me, and I just cannot believe that Tom is not with us. Sometimes he seems to be there leaning against the Welsh dresser, smiling round at us all in his gentle way.

When Justyn was in British Columbia, in a remote village, he received the message from New York of Tom's passing. He never even considered what to do, it was as though he had already had his commission. Without considering his flying job, or the work he was doing, he went to New York then flew to Hildenborough and shouldered the work that he and Tom had planned in such detail.

The generosity of hundreds of friends enabled Hildenborough Hall to be secured as a memorial to Tom. Already much of the plan has been put into operation; extra bedrooms are being built, the kitchens reorganised, but best of all young people are finding their way to Hildenborough, particularly on the Monday night Open House, not for entertainment, but to sit down with a Bible in their hand to see what God has to say to them.

Our happy time of retirement never came, but it would be foolish to imagine that we would ever have lived happily together like Darby and Joan. Our dream was of a bungalow, with a studio for me to paint in; a workshop where Tom would use his tools; but if I am honest, I know exactly what would have happened. I would be cooking something very tasty, and Tom would come in to see me with a guilty look, and say, 'Leave all that, and come for a walk. I want to talk something over, I've got an idea.' Out would come his stick, and Tom would say, 'I want to build an old people's village, a dream place, for people who want their own home, but need care. We'll have an old world village green,' and I would add, 'Let's have a village shop where we can sell all the things old people want, wool for their knitting, and we must have a restaurant with beautiful recherché meals to tempt their appetites.' By the time we finished talking we would have planned every detail with enormous enthusiasm, to the colour of the paint on the cottage windows. We would go back, and while I reheated the casserole, Tom would be getting on to the house agents for details of large estates, and over his shoulder would say, 'And later on we would be able to live there ourselves.' 'We'd better get details of battery-operated bath chairs while you're on the phone,' I would say from the kitchen.

It is wonderful to think of being with Christ. One compensation for losing someone you love as much as I loved Tom is that death is a friend. I only feared death because it meant leaving him when he needed me.

I had a glorious realisation in the night a few days ago. I was praying, as I always do, in my waking moments, and suddenly realised that when I thought of death, it was not to be with Tom, but it was to be with Christ, which is far better—'joy unspeakable and full of glory'. The last verse of a poem I wrote recently says:

The practise of His presence here
Makes earth grow futile, heaven near,
And when the call to heaven will come
Our passing will be going Home.

After the Mission to Britain, Tom said, 'Rest? We have all eternity to rest.' I just don't believe it—for 'His servants shall serve Him'.

If God says to Tom, 'Rule over ten cities,' he will be in his element. I will be occupying my little hamlet, with plenty of time to spare, and Tom will say, 'Jean, come over to my capital, I've got a wonderful idea, I want to talk it over with you.'